*Twayne's United States Authors Series*

Sylvia E. Bowman, *Editor*

INDIANA UNIVERSITY

*Bernard DeVoto*

# BERNARD DeVOTO

By ORLAN SAWEY

*Pan American College*

 **151**

Twayne Publishers, Inc.   ::   New York

# Preface

ALTHOUGH Bernard DeVoto has been dead for more than twelve years, no full-length study of his contribution to American history and literature has been made. A good, though incomplete, bibliography has been published, along with portraits done by four of his friends. His writing deserves better treatment than personal evaluations by his friends or the necessarily limited treatment of him in this book. Moreover, his place in American letters needs a clearer definition.

One of the difficulties that DeVoto presents to anyone writing about him is his not fitting a pattern, especially a preconceived pattern of what a novelist, or historian, or critic ought to be. A few years ago a scholarly journal returned to me an article on DeVoto's novels and inadvertently included a comment by an eminent critic that the works discussed were "some very minor novels by a good historian but a mediocre popular novelist." For much of his life, in spite of the critic's comment, DeVoto considered himself a novelist (although he was never a popular one); and my historian friends tend to disparage his historical works because of their popularity and, perhaps, their interest.

Then, too, DeVoto stirred up enough controversy among literary critics for him to be considered one of them, although this statement would cause him pain. He probably did more than any other person to focus attention on Mark Twain as a representative American writer. But he was frequently unfriendly to the critics.

DeVoto was more like William Dean Howells than like any other American writer. Howells was a journalist with a wide range of interests, typically shown in *Harper's* the "Editor's Easy Chair," which he wrote for twenty years and one month. DeVoto wrote the "Easy Chair" for twenty years and three months. Both men observed and commented freely on all aspects of American life, in *Harper's* and in other journals. Both were belletrists.

Howells was one of the few American writers who moved from the frontier to the East, made adjustment to a new-found prosperity, and still wrote mature literature. Hamlin Garland failed to do this, as have many others. DeVoto defended his own writing for the slicks, but his love for the history of his native West inspired writing far above the slick level.

The purpose of this work is to trace DeVoto's development as a writer by tracing the element most common to most of his major works: his love for the American West and his presentation of his ideas about it. The Westward Movement was a vital force in American writing, either positively or negatively. Although DeVoto's love for the West dominated his writing, he had no patience with those who romanticized the Western experience and "the American Dream." He wrote realistically about the frontier. In his novels, his histories, and his critical works he insisted on fact; he was merciless towards those who romanticized the Western saga; he was equally merciless in his damning of those men and enterprises which sought to exploit and to destroy the remaining natural resources.

The main sources of this study have been the major published works of Bernard DeVoto, the ones he thought enough of to publish under his own name. I have read only with passing interest novels and articles published under pseudonyms such as John August and Cady Hewes, and I have rejected them as not being pertinent to this study. I have not cited very many of his magazine articles, except those in *Harper's;* most of his other articles were reprinted in one or another of the collections of his essays.

It has been difficult not to digress from the main theme of this book, the influence of the frontier concept on American writing and American institutions, as seen in DeVoto's historical and literary theories and in his literary works. DeVoto was interested in many aspects of American life. I have quoted more DeVoto than one usually does in a book of this sort, but most of the quotations come at the end of long summaries. And often DeVoto cannot be paraphrased without loss of the essence of his ideas; he was not a wastrel with words. And the critical material, especially, is not readily available, although it should be.

It is at this point that an author generally acknowledges the help he has received in his work. I, of course, recognize that without the help of my wife, Nina, and of my daughter, Sara, I would not have had the time to work on this book. But I would also like to acknowledge one more indebtedness: to Bernard DeVoto himself, for helping me to get rid of at least one bad stylistic habit. After all, I could not very well write, "DeVoto devoted ten pages...."

ORLAN SAWEY

*Pan American College*
*Edinburg, Texas*

# Acknowledgments

I am grateful to Mrs. Bernard DeVoto for permission to quote from and to use the writings of Bernard DeVoto in the preparation of this book; she holds the copyrights to the DeVoto works. I am also grateful for her reading of the manuscript and for her comments on it. I would also like to make special acknowledgment to the Harvard University Press for permission to quote from *Mark Twain at Work*.

# Acknowledgments

# Contents

# Contents

# Chronology

1932 *Mark Twain's America.*

1934 *We Accept with Pleasure.*

1935 The first "Easy Chair" essay, November *Harper's* magazine. Essay each month until January, 1956.

1936 September 26 to March 1, 1938, editor of *Saturday Review of Literature. Forays and Rebuttals.*

1937 Litt. D., Middlebury College.

1938 Curator of Mark Twain papers until 1946.

1939 August, to Breadloaf School of English. Taught there several summers.

1940 *Minority Report.* Edited *Mark Twain in Eruption.*

1942 *Mark Twain at Work.* Litt. D., Kenyon College. Became member of editorial board of *New England Quarterly.*

1943 *The Year of Decision: 1846.*

1944 *The Literary Fallacy.*

1946 Edited *The Portable Mark Twain.*

1947 *Mountain Time* and *Across the Wide Missouri.* May, 1947, to May, 1948, editor of *America in Books,* monthly publication of History Book Club.

1948 Received Pulitzer Prize in history for *Across the Wide Missouri.*

1949 Appointed member of Advisory Board on National Parks.

1950 *The World of Fiction.*

1951 *The Hour.*

1952 *The Course of Empire.*

1953 Edited *The Journals of Lewis and Clark.* National Book Award for non-fiction.

1955 *The Easy Chair.* Died November 13.

1956 *Women and Children First* (by Cady Hewes).

## CHAPTER 1

# Beginnings: The Frontier as Myth

**B**ERNARD AUGUSTINE DeVOTO was born on January 11, 1897, at Ogden, Utah, the son of Florian Bernard and Rhoda Dye DeVoto; his father was an apostate Catholic and his mother an apostate Mormon. Arthur M. Schlesinger, Jr., says that his Western birth "gave him an identification with the experience of the frontier and a permanent concern with the process by which America became a continental nation."[1]

After one year at the University of Utah and three years at Harvard, DeVoto graduated from Harvard with Phi Beta Kappa honors in 1920, World War I having intervened (he was a lieutenant in the army and a stateside instructor in marksmanship). After graduation he spent two years planning a history of northern Utah, working on a ranch in Utah, and following the frontier trails to acquire background. Then, after teaching history for a year at Ogden Junior High School (1921-22), he became an instructor of English at Northwestern University from 1922 until 1927, when he resigned to make a living with his pen.[2]

## I  *Interpreter of the West*

Perhaps this bare sketch of the beginnings of one of America's best-known writers sheds little light on the man himself, but it shows that DeVoto's background, unlike that of Howells, the American writer whom he most resembles, is an academic background. Product of the West and of Harvard College, he did not permit whatever schism there was between the two to turn him aside from the purpose which controlled most of his serious writing: the full interpretation of the Westward Movement and its influence on the forming of the American empire.

During his years at Evanston, DeVoto wrote numerous book reviews for the *Evanston News-Index*, the *Chicago Post*, and the

*Saturday Review of Literature*, a controversial article on Utah for the *American Mercury* (as well as other articles for the same magazine), and articles for *Harper's*. In addition, he wrote a novel, "Crock Crow," still unpublished; published two novels; worked on a third novel (published in 1928); and, incidentally, helped write a freshman composition text.[3]

## II  *Western Novelist*

While at Northwestern, in the midst of these other activities, DeVoto began writing novels. In all, he published five under his own name. In spite of the comments of his friends and enemies to the contrary, DeVoto always considered himself a novelist, though not always a popular or successful one. The dates of his novels (his last was published in 1947) indicate his continued interest in fiction.

As a novelist, DeVoto continually sought to explain the West to his readers. Of his first five novels— *The Crooked Mile* (1924), *The Chariot of Fire* (1926), *The House of Sun-Goes-Down* (1928), *We Accept with Pleasure* (1934), and *Mountain Time* (1947)—the first three deal with the Western Movement and the influence of the frontier on American civilization. The fourth, *We Accept with Pleasure*, describes the intellectual life in the East of some of the relatives of John Gale, DeVoto's frontier historian; and it contrasts the effete Eastern civilization with the more meaningful life of the West (or at least the Middle West). The fifth, *Mountain Time*, is partially set in the West. The basic theme, the redemption found in separation from the degrading forces of the East, is in keeping with DeVoto's general attitude.

When Frederick Jackson Turner read a paper entitled "The Significance of the Frontier in American History" before the American Historical Association in 1893, he changed the thinking of American historians. American history since that time has been influenced, either directly or indirectly, by Turner's theories on the importance of the frontier in the development of American democracy and individual freedom. During the past sixty years Turner's ideas have been attacked severely and defended staunchly. Historians have elaborated on and sometimes perverted his ideas with sectarian zeal and glee. Others have attacked his thesis with equal ardor. In the midst of the controversy DeVoto wrote his novels about the American frontier. Relatively unknown, the novels are significant revelations of DeVoto's ideas.

The first novel, *The Crooked Mile*, a careful study of the frontier town of Windsor, shows the deterioration in the third generation of a frontier family, the Abbeys, and describes the new West, a West controlled by rapacious corporations which have destroyed or at least emasculated the frontier ideal. The second novel, *The Chariot of Fire*, pursues a side issue, frontier religion, in a description of the religious fanatic previously written about by William Dean Howells in *The Leatherwood God*. The third novel, *The House of Sun-Goes-Down*, describes the earlier phases of frontier development as seen in the lives of the first two Abbeys and in the history of a frontier town, Windsor.

Although DeVoto's general theme is the validity of the frontier ideal, he is more interested in an analysis of the mind of the frontiersman than in the pursuit of a historical thesis. He never forgets that he is a novelist, writing about real people. His novels are intellectual; he develops his main characters—Pemberton Abbey, Gordon Abbey, John Gale, and Hope Gale—by tracing their thinking and reproducing their conversations. Action is slowed by long philosophical discussions; but, at the same time, character is more clearly revealed. After all, people do discuss ideas, sometimes at boring lengths. But DeVoto succeeds admirably in avoiding boredom.

### III   *The Abbey Family*

In DeVoto's novels the Westward Movement is revealed in the lives of men of three generations of the Abbey family. The frontier is shown as a place of hardships and problems. The wife of James Abbey, the patriarch of the Abbey family, never became reconciled to frontier life. The struggle in the first generation was against the land itself; in the second generation, against the encroachment of a tainted capitalism; in the third generation, against a highly-organized, dominant capitalism. In DeVoto's plots violence is minimized, and human relationships are emphasized. Few Western novelists have as clearly avoided the usual clichés about Western life.

The first Abbey, James, went to the frontier from the South of the Reconstruction. Discontent, individualistic, proud, he went to the West to be free. Only grudgingly did he cooperate with his neighbors. His entire life was devoted to the land, which he loved profoundly. Despite several opportunities to amass wealth, he consistently refused to be a businessman. For a time, he operated a sawmill with Herman Kleinfeld; but his dislike of commerce aided Kleinfeld in bilking him. James believed in the land; his resources were depleted in a quixotic attempt to settle new land, the Grouse Creek Basin; and he died a failure.

DeVoto pictures James Abbey as a typical and dogged pioneer, but not necessarily an idealistic one. Father Tierney, frontier priest of Windsor, described him as having "that fire in the heart that sends smoke to the brain."[4] The search of the pioneer for the intangible, the search for freedom, is shown in James Abbey, who is typical of many pioneers who "don't find their homes on earth nor in heaven, nor yet in hell."[5] His restless discontent is typical of that which motivated many who went West.

James Abbey's only legacy to his son, Pemberton, was a dislike of farming; but Pemberton wasted no time in becoming wealthy. He taught himself engineering and became a mining expert. His first real money was made by piracy; finding a flaw in the title of tycoon Mordecai Krug's most valuable mine, he extorted a million dollars from Krug. He joined Herman Kleinfeld (in a later generation, Littlefield) in a project to bring drinking water to Windsor. When Abbey wanted to form irrigation projects, Kleinfeld refused; and Abbey sold out, turning to the "Abbey process" of smeltering low-grade ore. Defeated by Eastern capitalists and by his own nonconformity (he was betrayed by his partner, the brother of his mistress), Pemberton left very little to his son, Gordon. So the basic problem of *The Crooked Mile* is whether Gordon would, like the rest of the third-generation Windsorites, become a wastrel, a degenerate traitor to the frontier individualism of his forebears, or would help in the development of the land and thus fight the encroaching capitalism, the enemy of the agrarian and mining frontiers.

## IV  *John Gale, Frontier Historian*

One of DeVoto's main problems was to arrive at a method of

discussing facets of frontier philosophy and still to write a novel. The conventions of the modern novel discourage long digressions for the purpose of discussing ideas. DeVoto partially solved this problem by removing John Gale, contemporary of Pemberton Abbey, from his native New England and setting him down in Windsor, where he devoted most of his life to writing a history of the frontier. DeVoto used excerpts from these imaginary histories as introductions to sections of *The Crooked Mile*. He had Pemberton Abbey, Gordon Abbey, and other characters in the novels discuss Gale's writing with him. In these discussions, a natural part of the novels, the various concepts of the frontier emerge. The frontier complex is seen through the eyes of John Gale:

A band of prospectors wintering by necessity at the mouth of Windsor Canyon beside the hot-pot spring, had begun the story. Hi-Yi Windsor, prospector, gambler, gold-washer, and merchant, had found that the distempers of his flesh were allayed by the hot water, had set up a store where desert rats and freighters who strayed from the Overland trail might find refreshment, or might risk and lose the dust they had acquired. Then the Florence fields two hundred miles away had burst into flower and Hi-Yi's station became their source of supply. Followed a mushroom growth, saloons, honky-tonks, gambling houses—an incorporated city with five thousand people and a populous cemetery and Mayor Windsor in silk hat and flowered waistcoat welcoming the distinguished at its corporate limits. Windsor's Boiling Springs City was its name then, a title which contracted toward the center with every change of phase. Florence passed; Helena got more direct access to freight supplies; the gamblers and the harlots departed; Hi-Yi became a mayor without constituency and sold grain and farmlands and lottery-tickets on the side. Then the railroad and the homesteaders, bringing a double slavery; for what the railroads did not possess, the banks that followed in its wake soon took over.

There, till the end of time, Windsor would have rested. The brief rebellion of Henry Clay Bryce, the farmers recrudescent, had shown that the frontier had constructed its own damnation. But Pemberton Abbey burrowed into the mountains and brought back his worthless copper salts, which in due time the Abbey Process transmuted into a new power. Here was the one chance that Windsor had ever had to break free. And Windsor, obeying the instinct of the Gadarene swine, had stampeded into the sea.

Windsor, united, had crushed Pemberton Abbey, and in his death had enslaved itself forever, past any hope of liberation. With the coming of Pemberton's successors, the copper barons of the east, Windsor was doomed.[6]

Typical of DeVoto's long and involved philosophical conversations in *The Crooked Mile* is this discussion of John Gale and his frontier history by Gordon Abbey in a conversation with Hope Gale:

> John Gale doesn't justify a biography except as a mind. You would begin with the clipper ships and what the Civil War did to Boston. Then you would consider the last decay . . . the deliquescence of puritanism. The Nation and The Statesman and James Russell Lowell and Eliot, while the trusts came up like thunder and the Irish washed over the dam. All this before you said a word about your father. And at the same time you would have to summarize the frontier—discovery, exploitation, colonization, the ox-teams, the nesters, the railroad, the mines, the banks, populism, free silver, my father. For you would have to pass judgment on your father's work. John Gale had only one idea, ultimately, and you would have to show less what it meant than what it sprang from. And you would have to end with the book he never wrote, the one he was leading up to—the apocalypse. Last Days, the damnation of the human race, a damnation which either resulted from the landing of the Mayflower or was inherent in protoplasm when the original blobs coalesced in the sea.[7]

DeVoto even provided John Gale with a fictional bibliography, a quite believable one. The first volume was entitled *The Goisute Indians* (1897); its subtitle indicates that it was a discussion of the organization, culture, and folklore of an American tribe. The work of Gale's most often quoted by DeVoto is *The Diaspora: A History and Criticism of the Frontier Movement in America.* Volumes I and II were published in Boston by the Laurel Press in 1908 and volumes III and IV by the same press in 1910. *The Frontier Ethos: Essays in Western History* was published in 1911 and *Religious Colonization: A Study of Catholic and Calvinistic Civilization in Western America* in 1914. Gale also published a biography of the great populist, Henry Clay Bryce, but this date of publication is unknown.[8]

These "histories" considerably add to the realism of DeVoto's frontier novels. They serve as a basis for questioning the impor-

tance of the frontier in American civilization. DeVoto made Gale
an iconoclast, a New England puritan who ruthlessly pushed
aside romantic concepts of the frontier and described social development from the detached viewpoint of the scientific historian. DeVoto said of Gale that he laid forever the myth that
human freedom had any more existence on the frontier than elsewhere. He had Gale say that the frontier was only a ghost, that
most frontiersmen blindly obeyed necessity, and that frontiers of
courage and of creation never existed—they were only mysterious
and occult delusions.

Although Louis Farrand, Gale's son-in-law, believed that "the
kingdom of heaven was in process of establishment on the frontier" and that all that remained was the education of certain
politicians, John Gale's books announced that no millennium
would spring from the frontier; energy had declined. Gale insisted that the pioneer was "not a superman dominated by visions
of empire, but a hell-ridden calvinist driven west by economic
pressure." Moreover, "Not God's whisper urged him out, but
bankruptcy among his stronger brothers. He sought not something lost behind the ranges, but free land by which he might
repair his fortunes."[9]

In the introduction to Part II of *The Crooked Mile* DeVoto
quoted from *The Diaspora,* making Gale insist that there was
no real frontier—there was no freedom, opportunity, and virtue;
there was "only an advancing fringe of dubious civilization
where men repeated the unchanging cycle of their race. There
were inheritors of fear and barrenness and frustration."[10]

## V   The Chariot of Fire

In the same quotation Gale gave the example of Job Rutherby,
who for twenty years preached that life was a dream; later,
Rutherby added to this doctrine the conviction that he was the
author of the dream. Before the truth of this claim was fully
established, however, he left hurriedly when he was informed
that a marshal was bringing a warrant charging him with cattle
rustling. This story of Gale's provided the theme of DeVoto's
second novel, *The Chariot of Fire,* the story of the religious
fanatic Ohio Boggs, who finally decided that he was God. The
novel is indeed a picture of the "barrenness and frustration"

which to a considerable extent motivated the religion of the frontier.

In *The Chariot of Fire* DeVoto gave a memorable picture of the pioneer, the frontiersman, in the person of Lias Whipple and his companion, who came to Elam, a frontier settlement, to find Jesus and found Ohio Boggs instead:

> They were strangers, yet their twins might be living along any of the four roads that led to Elam. They had the low forehead and the wide, stooped shoulders of the pioneer, the loose stride, the solemn mouth. They were of the race that was rising from the Mississippi to the Gulf to restore freedom and to bring the republic into being, to drive out the bootlicking Adams and to elevate Jackson the Liberator. They were the people; the new America. . . . But these two—there was something obstinate and strange in their bewilderment. . . . Dust overlay their doeskin shirts, their breeches and leggings, their thick boots, had even found its way under the fur caps which they had removed in the presence of gentry. But their eyes were level in spite of dust and weariness . . . it was plain they had come through dust and heat on extraordinary business.[11]

DeVoto described a part of the frontier conflict in Jeff Brashear:

> Jeff was heavy-jawed and heavy-handed, a dull, powerful man who worked his way uncertainly among the pitfalls of this world. The best settler in the vicinity—the best log-roller, rail-splitter, roof-raiser, timber-clearer—he had been tormented all his life by a fear of damnation. He drank not at all, and was but little given to the ways of the world, but his days were often black with the remembrance of his sins.[12]

Another type of frontiersman was Joe Stevens, an ex-riverman who might have originated in the pages of Twain's novels. He is typical of the "half-horse, half-alligator" later portrayed by Franklin J. Meine in *Tall Tales of the Southwest* and by DeVoto in *Mark Twain's America:*

> Joe Stevens' voice bellowed over the countryside like the whistle of the steamboat he was imitating.
> "Wahoo! Wahoo! Six-foot shoal off the port bow. Bateau runnin' under the bows. Wahoo! Wahoo! Get 'at bateau from under, Judge, or you'll get slit in two and ride my wash to ever-

lasting glory. I'm burnin' pitch! I'm walkin' on my paddles! Wahoo! Look out, bateau."[13]

One of the most memorable characterizations in *The Chariot of Fire* is that of the village atheist, Thomas Chadbourne, "a bewildering infidel," always on the side of religious freedom. Chadbourne, dubbing the camp meeting an "orgy" and attributing the craziness of a pioneer family who burnt their old grandmother as a sacrifice to their having just attended a camp meeting, spoke of the power of a similar camp meeting:

> A man could feel it with his skin. It might, I say, set a torch to Elam. Or string you or me from a tupelo. Or make matrons of a hundred maids. . . . These people glorifying their creator had a striking similarity to the Winnebagoes on the dance before the warpath. They woo God by spasms and win him by delirium. They worship him by clattering their bones together in terror; they exalt him by rolling in agony through the mud. Surely he did not lie who wrote they were made in his image.[14]

## VI   *The Frontier of Reality*

DeVoto's frontiersmen were not romanticized. He did not subscribe to what he considered perversions of the Turner thesis. On the title page to Part I of *The Crooked Mile*, John Gale commented clearly on the influence of the frontier and the frontier concept:

> At the hands of poets, professors, and Presidents, two myths have developed, the Pioneer and the Frontier. The Pioneer has become a composite of Tamur the Great and William of Normandy, a demi-god combining grandeur, statecraft, and prophecy in equal measure and following the inspiration of God in a conscious effort to magnify the glory of the race. The Frontier has become a transitory but already hallowed utopia where, uniquely in human history, individualism was supreme and freedom a universal endowment. . . . The pioneer, in his earliest phase, was a fugitive from justice and in his latest only a hellridden calvinist forced out by his economic helplessness and searching not for something lost behind the ranges but for free land. . . . Freedom was conditioned by the inheritance of the race, a heritage not devoid of injustice, mediocrity, tyranny, and fear. And the true individualist on the frontier is to be found at one end of a rope whose other end is in the hands of a group of vigilantes.[15]

Such was John Gale's theory of the frontier. What happened when this theory was applied to real situations? What was the effect of such a theory on the disillusioned human mind? Pemberton Abbey's early death left his friend John Gale responsible for the upbringing of Gordon Abbey. In thinking about Gordon and his education, Gale reflected that the frontier was a waste of men, wealth, and energy. But, when a good mind appeared in the third generation, should it be left to rot? Theoretically, this good mind, unless freed, ought to rend itself; but Gordon grew fat among swine. *The Diaspora*, a chronicle of decaying energies, had worked out a formula for the process of decay; but Gale was not comforted when Gordon chose to substitute himself for the unknown $X$ of the formula.[16]

So Gale tried to encourage Gordon to make something of himself. When he talked to Gordon, however, he received this reply: "I'm the third generation. I'm the fall of the house.... I can't hear the bugle calling, nor thirst for blood. The family has gone up Salt Creek—and I'm damned glad." But John Gale was sorry.[17]

After Gordon tried his hand at journalism in the East and became successful, he decided suddenly to return to the West. He wrote Gale that perhaps his Abbey blood required that he work out his salvation on Gale's mythical frontier. On the other hand, he reflected, it might be possible that his arteries were more flexible among the hills.[18] However, when Gordon returned to Windsor, he lapsed into lethargy. Gale, in an attempt to arouse him, raised for him the specter of the tyranny of Eastern capitalism. Gordon had already insisted that the frontier had disappeared in the third generation through the agency of the smelters and the Abbey process perfected by his father. Gale said,

"There have been tyrannies in the west before this. The cattlemen had one. It was broken by the homesteader. Then came the banks. It was broken by the homesteader. The present tyranny is the smelter interknit with the bank and the railroad. And it can be broken in the same way."

Gordon shouted, "I merely reverted from the Abbey contempt to an active millennium. But there sits *The Diaspora*, his life of Henry Clay Bryce not yet off the press, telling me to go back to the land."

"Of the earth we were made," Gale said equably, "and, no matter what I may write in books I have taken too seriously, we

were damned the moment we got away from it. Millions of acres
that a plow has never scratched. The moment they are scratched,
the tyranny of copper will evaporate."[19]

His theories to the contrary, Gale had succumbed to the idea
that salvation was to be found in the free land of the frontier.
He was making an effort to interest Gordon in settling the
Grouse Creek Basin, a project which had been the ideal of his
grandfather, James Abbey. Gordon became bitter at the idea of
John Gale, the elderly iconoclast who had forever destroyed the
frontier's glamour, now dreaming of a new frontier. Actually,
thought Gordon, the frontier had always existed, an intangible
and splendid life, the restless desire which had already consumed
two Abbeys. But he, Gordon, had no such desire; he was too
cynical.

Even when Gordon came into contact with Pierce Dunlap,
swinish son of Aaron Dunlap, the blacksmith and controller of
the smelters (Pierce was the husband of the woman Gordon
loved), he was not stirred. For a moment he had the desire to
destroy the combine by following Gale's advice and opening up
the Grouse Creek Basin, but cynicism prevailed. Later, Gordon
reflected that the remaining frontier was that of the mind. The
ability to be calm and cynical was itself a frontier. John Gale had
insisted that the other two Abbeys had resisted the weakness of
the frontier and that he, Gordon, should do the same. DeVoto
wrote:

> Gale's frontier had moved west, had crossed the last moun-
> tains, had presumably been drowned in the Pacific. The third
> Abbey had been led to the frontiers of the spirit, along whose
> edge he had wandered these twenty-eight years. . . .
> The four volumes of *The Diaspora* lay on his table as on
> Hope's: Gale's history of men who had believed, to their damna-
> tion, in something that did not exist. Gordon turned the pages of
> one volume as though to recall the canvas-tops plodding west-
> ward through the alkali dust in which Pemberton Abbey had
> been born, plodding westward under a white hot sun to a line
> of illusion where freedom was reported to exist for mankind.

John Gale's book was right. In Gordon Abbey the frontier
played its accustomed fugues. Canvas-tops pushing westward
peaks and deserts where men were to be free, were ignorantly
headed toward a mirage. And Gordon Abbey, in the manner of

his house, had labored through plagues and derision toward the same imaginary wilderness. In the four-volume history of John Gale . . . were the reasons why the illusion should persist. . . . He had no need of *The Diaspora*. . . . It sufficed that the place was at last seen to be imaginary. Frontiers, whether they were the parked wagons of an emigrant train or the aspiration of Gordon Abbey, did not exist. . . . Today he had made an end of them, buried them utterly away. The last frontier sank out of sight, the third Abbey gave up the pursuit of phantoms, and the fiction of an Abbey fire died. . . .

John Gale's book was right. The frontier, the boundary of freedom and manhood, was a mirage, something born of sun and silence, a chimera of the brain. And John Gale, the man, had been wrong. When he looked at the Abbeys and said that they were no part of it, that they were fire and force to oppose it and to do what it had never done, that the freedom never seen on the frontier had somehow come to dwell in them—he too fell victim to the inverted landscape on the sky.

Gordon dropped the four volumes of *The Diaspora* in his wastebasket. That lesson was learned.[20]

John Gale, the revised version, however, had the last say. When Gale died, Gordon found that his own personal fortune was largely imaginary, that Gale had supported him for years. He also found that most of Gale's money had been invested in building a railway to the Grouse Creek Basin. The Gale estate had gone to restore the frontier and thus to free the land from Eastern capitalism. Gordon, first shocked, then amused, then interested, finally joined forces with the builder of the railway and began to carry out Gale's plan.

DeVoto thus says that, while there is some truth to Gale's iconoclastic picture of the frontier, there actually was some freedom yet to be found on the frontier, freedom on the part of those who opposed the forces which sought to destroy the land. The land, thus, is ennobling. The first generation of the Abbeys, in the person of James Abbey, in developing the land set up the basis of the only freedom that was possible. Pemberton Abbey, his son, aided the coming in of industry, the railroads, and the banks; and he thus contributed to the slavery of the Westerner. Industrialism destroyed that which seemed (even though it may not have been) noble in the lives of the original settlers. Their descendants, the third generation, were corrupted. Even Gordon

Abbey was pictured as growing fat among swine. Where did redemption lie? In a return to the land. The fault did not lie in the land but in forces which had corrupted the frontier ideal.

## VII   We Accept with Pleasure

*We Accept with Pleasure* is one of DeVoto's better novels. Moreover, it is hard to understand why it has not received more attention. First, it is DeVoto's "lost generation" novel, one which pictures the unease of the era (as does *The Crooked Mile*) but which is neither as hopeless nor as sentimental about the post-World War I era as the books of Hemingway or Fitzgerald are. Second, its underlying themes indicate that the answer to the lost-generation problems lie not in the Brahminism and the dilettantism of the East but in the less corrupted Western civilization.

Two groups of characters dominate the action: the Gales and the Ewings, proper Bostonians and relatives of DeVoto's frontier historian John Gale; and the non-Bostonians, Libby and Ted Grayson of the academic world, and Ric Barreda, creator of hit plays and musicals. The characters are brought together by a mutual interest: all of the men served together in the same unit in the war, and all were close to Julian Gale, the heroic ideal of most of the group. Julian had died not in battle but of a fairly common disease soon after the war.

The complicated interrelationships of the characters need not be discussed here—nor can all the characters be treated. These relationships are made clear, and the characters are painstakingly individualized. They move, act, and reveal themselves in their reactions to the Sacco-Vanzetti case and its aftermath. The dead Julian Gale is always in the background.

Chief among the Bostonian Gales and Ewings were Jonathan Gale, a successful Boston lawyer who finally attempted to fill his empty life with politics; Gage Ewing, a cynical, satyric research physician; Hester Gale, the dead Julian's sister and mistress to Jonathan (she died tragically and young); Hester's father, Edward, who lived only for the memory of his son; Fanny Gale, female politician and Jonathan's eventual political sponsor; and Richard Ewing, a ruthless Boston financier who committed his brother Bland to an asylum because he wanted to give his inheritance to charity.

An outsider coming into the Eastern Gale society, besides the Graysons and Barreda, was Loring Gale, of the Chicago branch of the family. Loring, besides having served with Julian during the war, had edited a radical journal in Chicago. The entrance of the outsiders and the exit of some of them provide the basic theme of the novel.

Loring Gale, representing perhaps the vigor of the Western society, entered into the Brahmin society and very soon was indistinguishable from the other Gales. He edited and published the letters of Julian Gale, even after he found out that Julian, whom all of his relatives and friends idolized, was a poser and a fake, that during the war he had pulled all the strings he could to be the commander of a squad which executed an enlisted man, merely to experience (and perhaps record) the thrill. Loring also wrote a history of his own decade, a popular history unworthy of his talents, published serially in a newspaper. He always intended to write a history of the influence of the West on American civilization (the purpose and the scope were vague), but the reader feels that the history was never written. Moreover, he finally married Beatrice Gale, his mistress and the ex-mistress of many others, including Gage Ewing and the synthetic Julian.

The Grayson family was brought to Boston because of Ted's loss of a teaching job at Northwestern University. Wounded war hero Grayson was accused of pacifism by an American Legion unit of arm-chair heroes and was fired by his department chairman, who, for sufficient reasons, already disliked him. Bothered by psychological problems, Ted had a nervous breakdown and was brought to the East by the Gales for treatment. He was cured, but his singing of the beautiful folk songs of the West was first exploited by Ric Barreda and eventually degraded by Barreda and Jewish composer, Misch Sachs, into a popular musical comedy. It was revealed in a conversation between Ted and Loren Gale that Ted had once soundly beaten Julian Gale because of the firing squad incident. Hatred of Julian was one of the reasons for Ted's problems. A part of Ted's cure was an affair with a chorus girl; and Libby, one of the more wholesome characters of the book, forced him to go back to teaching history at a college in the Midwest, thus escaping the destructive Eastern forces.

Obviously DeVoto meant to picture the Eastern branch of the lost generation as a decadent society. Its only hope was either politics (for Jonathan, a possible but doubtful hope) or the return to the purity of the Western climate. The ballads of the Western movement, beautiful and significant as sung by Ted Grayson, were degraded by contact with the Eastern culture, and became musical comedy material. The lost generation of the East was more lost than that of the West.

And then, DeVoto seems to say, the post-war era was confused because of misunderstanding and misplaced faith. Immediately after World War I Julian and his followers were going to save the world; but they failed. Ric, Loren, and Jonathan continually speculated about what Julian would have done if he had lived. All their failures and compromises were a result of Julian's not being there. Then, in revealing that Julian was miserably egocentric and small in spirit, DeVoto suggested that the idols of the lost generation really had no existence or reality. The only reality was the American experience, the American dream, the Westward movement of his early novels and later histories.

*We Accept with Pleasure* is a novel worthy of attention. It comments, though obliquely, on the American dream which is a part of most of DeVoto's writing. It is reflective of the love of the West seen in *Mark Twain's America* (1932) and in his later histories. It points toward DeVoto's later strong criticism of the critics who were unaware of the relation of literature to actuality, as seen in *The Literary Fallacy.*

Moreover, *We Accept with Pleasure* is a readable and interesting book that is frank in its picture of human relationships. The experiences of the Graysons at Northwestern are obviously autobiographical, and the reader senses that there is some of DeVoto in Loren Gale. Only when DeVoto attempts to provide a stream-of-consciousness view of the minds of some of his female characters is he tedious. Otherwise the novel deserves better treatment than it has been given.

## VIII Mountain Time

*Mountain Time* (1947), DeVoto's last and most popular novel, does not comment directly on the Western experience; but the basic theme is directly linked to the West. It is a better novel than many of those that followed World War II. The story opens in New York and concerns Cy Kinsman, resident surgeon of Mercy Hospital in New York, and Josephine Caneday Willard, the wife of would-be novelist Sam Willard, both natives of the Western town of Custis. Josephine, tired of supporting her writer husband and of his unfaithfulness to her, left him and took their daughter back to Custis. When Cy because of his honesty was forced out of his position by Dr. Alexander McAllister, the soul-less butcher who was his supervisor, he also went back to Custis where, having left the practice of medicine, he became a garage mechanic and rum runner. The townspeople, disgusted with the actions of Old Doc Kinsman's son, tried to rehabilitate him; but they did not succeed.

Cy's main interest was in helping Jo, whose life was complicated by psychological disorders; and gradually Jo's mental state improved. A part of her treatment was her singing, much of the time the old folk ballads, which DeVoto seemed to understand and appreciate, though one wonders why their singers are always the mentally disturbed. Eventually, even though Sam Willard became a successful novelist, Jo divorced him. And much later, after her cure, she finally married Sam, who took a job teaching physiology at the state "cow college."

The novel is similar to *We Accept with Pleasure*, but the characters are fewer and less complicated. DeVoto in essence says that the simple old days—those of Old Doc Kinsman, the frontier doctor, and Gideon Huntoon, pioneer cum business tycoon—were better. The forces of evil reside in the effete East. Sanity is found in the West and in Western life, where existence is still influenced by the frontier and is infinitely less complicated. Cy Kinsman of *Mountain Time* is very much like Gordon Abbey of *The Crooked Mile;* both were indecisive, and both solved their problems with compromise.

## IX   *The Value of DeVoto's Novels*

The question of whether DeVoto was a good novelist or not, or even whether or not he should even be considered a novelist, is controversial. Wallace Stegner, although admitting that the books are honest ones, states that the thrill of life is not in them. He feels that they are too contrived and perhaps too witty, too packed with ideas.[21] Others seem to agree with this evaluation, and even DeVoto was not always confident of his ability as a writer of mature fiction. It is true, however, that he always considered himself a fiction writer, although more and more as time went on he began to refer to himself as a historian. In 1937 he wrote an essay in the *Saturday Review of Literature* (reprinted in *Minority Report*) in which he said,

> Nevertheless the bulk of my writing is fiction—at least two-thirds of it. I have written serious fiction for my own pleasure and in the wistful but almost wholly frustrated hope that somebody else might like it. I have written light fiction to make a living; it has supported my family and my other writing (except for two years as editor of the *Saturday Review*) ever since July, 1927. I have written both light and serious fiction under my own name and under various aliases— and, such is the depravity of this world, it is only under my aliases that I ever get triple-starred or even single-starred in Mr. O'Brien's presentation lists. Criticism is always changing its taxonomy but if you classify a writer according to the thing he writes most, then I am a short story writer and a novelist.[22]

A year before, in 1936, he had referred to himself as a writer of novels "which few people read and fewer buy, light fiction for popular magazines, and social history of almost professional obscurity." He admitted, however, that the volume for which he was writing a preface (*Forays and Rebuttals*) proved that he had made considerable contributions to the "quality group" of magazines.[23]

DeVoto's novels have not received the place in literary history that they deserve. It is true that they are filled with ideas, but one should not be suspicious of them for this reason. DeVoto's fiction is especially valuable and interesting because of his unity of theme: explanation of the multi-faceted nature of the frontier experience, not from a romantic viewpoint but from an examination of the facts. One of these facts includes the psychological impact of Western freedom and openness. The healing of the wounds inflicted by the more complicated East may have been a part of the early frontier environment, even as it exists in reality in modern times.

The early novels show a preoccupation with the frontier, a desire to explain what happened there, that DeVoto never lost.

This interest embroiled him in controversy over Mark Twain and eventually led him into battle with other critics. His interest in frontier ways led to the writing of three full-length histories and many other essays on the West. It led into combat with the private-enterprise industrial forces which he felt had plundered the West and were attempting to continue to do so.

Finally, his experience as a fiction writer was a continual influence on DeVoto's other works. The narrative techniques of the novelist were used in *Mark Twain's America* and in the histories. The style of DeVoto, the historian, was continually being influenced by the imagination of DeVoto, the writer of fiction, although his love for "the facts" kept his imagination under strict control. Nevertheless, DeVoto's writing of novels has contributed greatly to the art and the interest of his histories.

## CHAPTER 2

# Editor and Critic: Mark Twain

## I  *Brooks and DeVoto*

IN 1920, Van Wyck Brooks, the eminent literary critic, wrote *The Ordeal of Mark Twain,* in which he used great imagination, dramatic techniques, and Freudian psychology to picture Twain as a shrinking genius, driven to success by a promise made to his mother on the night of his father's death and harassed by his rude, rough, uncouth frontier environment. This book was a milestone in Mark Twain criticism. DeVoto said that between 1920 and 1932, when *Mark Twain's America* was in galley proofs, Brooks's ideas had dominated all criticism of Mark Twain and had founded a school of literary criticism.[1]

In 1920 DeVoto was just finishing Harvard. By 1932 he had taught history at Ogden High School, English at Northwestern, and writing at Harvard. He had written three frontier novels and had reviewed numerous books. He had written articles for *Harper's, Saturday Review of Literature, American Mercury,* and other magazines; he had sold short stories to the *Saturday Evening Post* and *Redbook;* and he had become editor of *The Harvard Graduates' Magazine.* Many of the reviews were of books about Western America, and some of the articles were about the West. Among the other articles were several on Mark Twain, works which were later incorporated into *Mark Twain's America.*[2] Since he had begun the book several years before its publication,[3] the articles evidently grew out of the writing of the book.

DeVoto called his fourth book an "essay in the correction of ideas." He denied that it was social history, saying that it was not sufficiently comprehensive. He denied that it was biography; his interest had not been biographical. He denied that it was literary criticism, saying "that department of beautiful thinking is too insulated from reality for my taste." After reiterating that he wished to correct false ideas that had been set forth about Mark Twain, DeVoto concluded that perhaps the most honest way to classify the work was to say that it was the kind of book he had always wanted to write about Mark Twain.[4]

## II   Mark Twain's America

The effect of *Mark Twain's America* and of the Twain articles cannot be overestimated. In 1932, announcement was made that *The Ordeal of Mark Twain* was being revised; and Brooks's publishers indicated that some of the original ideas were to be reversed in the second edition.[5] Currently, when one mentions Van Wyck Brooks to a Mark Twain buff, he has to say, "Excuse me." And DeVoto's fine introduction to *The Portable Mark Twain* (1946) made only a passing allusion to the controversy: "The critic who for a moment forgets that Mark was a humorist is betrayed."[6] Brooks's theories were no longer influential. DeVoto's defense of Mark Twain as a robust American writer, product of the frontier, succeeded; no longer was Mark Twain regarded as a disappointed and frustrated Shelley.

*Mark Twain's America* produced what was perhaps an unexpected result for DeVoto. When DeVoto began studying Mark Twain, Albert Bigelow Paine, friend and biographer of Mark Twain, was literary executor of the Mark Twain papers. When DeVoto approached him for permission to look at the unpublished material, Paine firmly refused him. After all, DeVoto wrote, Paine's six-pound official biography had established the canon. Paine informed DeVoto that nothing more need *ever* be written about Mark Twain. DeVoto blackmailed him by submitting a series of questions unanswered by the biography and then threatening to publish "the best ascertainable rumors" if the questions were not answered.

In *Mark Twain's America* DeVoto complained about Paine's handling of the papers, asserting that he had no confidence in Paine's literary judgments. He suggested to the Clemens heirs that opening Mark Twain's unpublished manuscripts to research would not be sacrilege, and he listed several works that needed examination: "Mr. Paine, though a formidably good biographer, is something less than infallible as a critic; no one else has seen these manuscripts; yet, obviously, they must be accounted for. Public benevolence constrains me to offer the estate my services.[7] Six years later, in 1938, DeVoto himself became curator of the Mark Twain papers and continued in the position until 1946.

Besides various articles, usually later incorporated into prefaces and books, DeVoto, as curator of the Mark Twain papers, edited *The Adventures of Tom Sawyer* with a preface (1939), *Mark Twain in Eruption* with an introduction (1940), and *The Adventures of Huckleberry Finn* with an introduction (1942); wrote *Mark Twain at Work* (1942); and edited *The Portable Mark Twain* with an introduction (1946). DeVoto's most important critical works on Mark Twain also include two speeches (both published in *Forays and Rebuttals* in 1936). One of these was "Mark Twain: The Ink of History," an address given at the Mark Twain Centennial celebration in Columbia, Missouri, on December 6, 1935; the other was "Mark Twain and the Limits of Criticism," a paper read before the Modern Language Association on January 1, 1936.

### III   *The Frontier and Frontier Humor*

Thus DeVoto involuntarily entered the field of literary criticism because of his interest in the frontier. In 1930, as general editor of Knopf's "American Deserta Series," he had a part in the publication of Franklin J. Meine's *Tall Tales of the Southwest,* one of the classic collections of humorous sketches of the Old Southwest. Meine published Twain's "The Squatter and the Dandy" in the volume. DeVoto's opposition to Brooks and his group was based on their ignorance of the frontier, especially of frontier humor; and he set out, with great energy, to make them wise.

His basic theses in *Mark Twain's America* were that Mark Twain must be studied as a humorist and that, to understand him one must understand the frontier. Many who wrote about the frontier, he said, had neither lived on nor studied frontier America. DeVoto made it plain, however, that he had no "simple, unified formula" to explain Twain and that he had refused to answer many questions about him because he had no facts to base his theories on. He wrote,

I do not believe in simplicities about art, artists, or the subjects of criticism. I have no theory about Mark Twain. It is harder to conform one's book to ascertainable fact than to theorize, and harder to ascertain facts than to ignore them. In literature, beautiful simplicities usually result from the easier method, and, in literature, the armchair assertion that something must be true is the begetter of unity. One who is not content with assertion must usually be prepared to do without the unity also. . . . But the literary have fallen out of the habit of reading Mark Twain's books, on the ground that they are humorous or popular or repressed, and so the literary may find the first preface to them informative. My hope is that they will hereafter understand the desirability of reading his books before passing judgment on them.[8]

Although DeVoto claimed that he had no theory about Mark Twain, he had just stated the basic thesis of his book: in order to understand Mark Twain one had to understand the American frontier that produced him. At the same time that he derided the critics and claimed not to be one of them, he wrote the first really significant criticism of Mark Twain; and all sane critics of Mark Twain's works since 1932 have of necessity been influenced by *Mark Twain's America*. Also, there emerged in the writing of the Mark Twain book the method which was to guide DeVoto in his other works—the gathering of facts, and the basing of conclusions on facts rather than on emotional reaction.

Eight years after the publication of *Mark Twain's America*, in a preface which was continued in the middle of *Minority Report*, DeVoto answered Edmund Wilson's statements that he lacked understanding of Mark Twain: "If Mr. Wilson will glance at my book about Mark Twain with this in mind [that "one must place a forked stick over a higher truth and set up a yell for the facts"] he will observe that I there pinned down a higher truth with a forked stick and yelled for the facts. A number of the brethren have denounced that book in the eight years since it was published, but there has not yet been a single appeal from the facts it presents."[9]

DeVoto also, while making fun of the critics, set forth a principle that is the most important one to emerge from the "New Criticism" then developing at Vanderbilt, Chicago, and elsewhere: literature must be studied from the text itself. He insisted that to know Mark Twain one must read his books. While Brooks and Warren have mellowed somewhat and have permitted biography and history to be at least a part of criticism (compare the first and third editions of *Understanding Poetry*), others have insisted that a work of art must be studied separate from time and place. DeVoto would (and did) disagree violently with this theory.

Whether by design or not, DeVoto had become a literary theorist (he had been a critic for years, although he merely considered himself a book reviewer). In *Minority Report* he wrote, "How did I become a literary critic? Since the boys will not permit me to define criticism as reviewing that is continued in the back of the magazine, I must maintain that I have never been one."[10] And later he wrote, "That is why the Easy Chair prefers to be called a historian and why, when referred to as a critic, it insists that epithet be accompanied by a smile."[11]

With the writing of *Mark Twain's America* DeVoto also became a historian of the frontier, developing a historical method based on the accumulation and analysis of facts. But one must always keep in mind DeVoto's ideas about the importance of frontier America. He believed that one should not speak of the frontier's "tastes and interests and preferences." He saw the frontier as many different places in many stages of development, inhabited by people of many different cultures, degrees of intelligence, races, family traditions, and individual capacities. Many kinds of frontier existed, populated by people living many kinds of lives.[12] DeVoto did not believe in oversimplification, nor did he believe that it was always necessary to arrive at a conclusion in any study. All evaluations should be tentative.

The purpose of *Mark Twain's America* has been given: to show that Mark Twain and his "art" were typical of the real frontier America of Frederick Jackson Turner, not of the romanticist's frontier. DeVoto wrote: "In [Brooks's] analysis of Mark Twain the eidolon 'Frontier' has a primary importance; yet Mr. Brooks fails to consider Frederick Jackson Turner's study of the frontier, the basis of realism in any discussion, and there is no evidence that he ever heard of it or of the investigations it begot. He had no knowledge of the frontier and considered none essential."[13]

About the notions held by the critics DeVoto was positive; most of them were wrong. He wrote:

Annotation is essential. The Missouri in which the infant's [Clemens'] eyes opened was frontier, and that it was frontier is the whole truth about the books of Mark Twain. But the word "frontier" has passed into the custody of the ideologues, whose notions have marvelously distorted it. . . . Necessarily Samuel Clemens was a leaf that took its color from the sun; the sun of Florida [Missouri] and Hannibal shone on the Western rural slaveholding communities near the fringe of settlement during years when a boundless vigor was making America something it had not been, something not reducible to formula. Theories cluster. Opinions about that western fringe, those years, that vigor, and that America make an abundance of systems, canons for the orthodox whose distressing quality is that they cannot all be true. Conflict produces a residue, a literary notion: that it was all pretty detestable. . . .

A literary theory is a form of metaphysical autobiography. It permits its contriver to reconstruct facts in harmony with his prepossessions. . . . The theorist must show that what he alleges as fact has some correspondence in reality and he must be capable of distinguishing between facts and emotions about them.

Literary opinion fails to approve the frontier. On evidence not submitted, the frontier folk are held to be Puritans given to a rigid suppression of emotion and particularly sexual emotion which produced camp meetings, lynchings, and sexual debauch. Also, the Puritans were disciples of Rousseau, who had moved west with an idea of sucking at nature's breast doctrines of primitive perfection and finding in the wilderness an age of innocence conducted by the noble savage. A Calvinist thus becomes an infidel philosopher and the relations of his fathers with the Iroquois were fraternal. The perceptible incompatibles, however, cause no embarrassment, for it is also to be charged against frontiersmen that they offered no encouragement whatever to artists, neglecting to praise "Moby Dick" and "Leaves of Grass" a generation before they were written. They were extroverted, they suppressed individuality, they obeyed the dreadful compulsions of the herd, they were barren of art, they scourged their souls with Old Testament terrors. Above all, they were universally a repressed people who feared joy and pleasure, living out their lives in gloom. And further, the land they lived in was repellent.

For a moment, the land, urban America, developing a generation of urban theorists, has found its sentiments condemning rural America. One wonders why an environment held to be commendable for Thoreau is thought unfortunate for Mark Twain.[14]

## IV  *Frontier Pleasures*

The theorists had pictured the frontiersman as joyless, but the frontiersman neglected to follow the theory. Badger fights, bear baiting, cockfights, horseraces, and shooting matches were plentiful. Show boats puffed up and down rivers, and itinerant actors acted "masterpieces for the approval of Calvinists before smoky oil lamps in the lofts above crossroads stores." The Negro minstrel show developed, including Christy's Minstrels from which, DeVoto says, Mrs. Stowe lifted her atrocious Negro dialect, "making it more abominable as perhaps a saintly woman must."[15]

Moreover, the frontiersmen brought a folk art westward. The Scotch ballads were sung by the people of Garland's Dutcher's Coolly, and catgut strings were a part of the Western fur trade. The fur trapper carried his fiddle with him. Corn shuckings and roof raisings produced fiddle and banjo music. Fiddling contests were "as enjoyable as camp meetings." Old tunes and words were adapted to new events, and occasional ballads celebrated tragedies and larceny. Mainly the traditional ballad made its westward migration with those whom the critics called Puritans. The Negro spiritual was frequently heard on Twain's frontier.[16]

In spite of all this activity, now thoroughly documented (Cecil Sharpe made his collections of mountain ballads two or three years before Brooks's book was published), Brooks insisted that none of it existed! DeVoto quotes him as saying that America was a nation "that had no folk-music, no folk-art, no folk-poetry, or next to none, to express it, to console it."[17] After examining some statements about the influence of Puritanism on the pioneer—made by Brooks, Lewis Mumford, and Waldo Frank—DeVoto concluded, "A critical theory is a notion which may be converted to the assault of what one dislikes, and to submit a sentiment to the correction of fact is unquestionably an irrelevance. Thus to inquire what a theorist means by 'Pioneer,' 'Puritan,' or 'frontier,' or to request evidence of suppression of emotion, fear of sex, the non-existence of folk art, anaesthesia to loveliness, or any other villainy charged against the Puritan-Pioneer, would be to commit rudeness."[18] Frequently DeVoto cited the works of the Southern pre-war humorists, whose works were published in Meine's anthology, to show that the frontier was neither sex-starved nor emotionally suppressed.

## V   *The Roughness of the Frontier*

The tender-minded critics recoiled from frontier life because it was not concerned with "loveliness, perfect societies, or New Jerusalem." DeVoto admitted the presence of the uncouth on the frontier but said that the Westward Movement, a manifestation of Darwin's "impersonal selection, discarded them without rancor and without pity." About these people, comparable to those Missourians whom the people of Illinois called Pukes, DeVoto wrote:

> They were everywhere a thin deposit on society, an interpene-trating influence. The tide passed over the Appalachians; its re-jectamenta there were called "mountain whites." It passed through the forests, where the discard remained "pinywoods people." In the canebrakes they were "clay eaters"; along the turbid waters, "river rats." Generically, they were "squatters." The term at first implied admiration, for it signified people who had outdistanced the surveyors and had driven a stake into land that no one had claimed. It passed, with a lessening commenda-tion, to those who upheld the right of pioneers against absentee owners of land patents. Then the tide swept by and, without praise, a squatter was one whom the tide had left to rot amidst refuse on the beach. Literature knows them chiefly under the name of a Missouri county a few miles down the river from Hannibal: the Pike County Man.[19]

DeVoto, in his discussion of the Pike County Man pictured by Mark Twain, said that these people were the wreckage of the frontier, the product of poverty, hookworm (the result of the absence of privies), malaria, cholera, and dysentery. He sug-gested that the frontiersman probably had, constantly, about one degree of fever. This fever, he said, might explain many of the insanities emanating from the frontier, such as "holiness, or green-backery, . . . anti-rents furor, or populism, or prohibition." Fever, not Puritanism, was the source. This thesis, he felt, needed to be pursued by historians.[20]

Mark Twain, DeVoto said, grew up in this society filled with violence; it is significant that his first literary effort, "The Dandy Frightening the Squatter," was a humorous story contributed to a humorous newspaper, the *Carpet-Bag*. Twain, according to DeVoto, was the natural product of the real frontier society; and his writing grew out of the first realistic literature of America, the humor of the Old Southwest. His writing cannot be explained without taking the realities of the frontier, including its humor and its lighter moments, into account.[21]

## VI   *The Far Western Frontier*

In his chapter on "The River" DeVoto stated that the Great Valley was the center of a frontier that was passing during the years that Sam Clemens was a pilot on the Mississippi. When the Civil War destroyed the river trade, Clemens went west to Nevada with his brother Orion. There the frontier was at the "noon mark." Again Clemens became engrossed in the frontier; he merged with the part of the Westward Movement which jumped the Great Plains. It was the frontier which still remembered the mountain man; it was the frontier at its highest peak of development. DeVoto wrote of the mining era:

> The frontier was American energy in its highest phase. Here on the eastern slope of Sun Mountain it attained a final incandescence. The sulphurets of silver created an era at once unique and a consummation. Great wealth in hard rock and speculative stocks, the chaos of frontiersmen seeking it, the drama of their conflicts, the violence of their life, the spectacle of their pleasures, and above all the rhythm of destiny shaping the national experience—there seems no reason to deplore this. It was the end and fulfillment of a process that had begun on a gaunt shingle where Plymouth woods met the December sea. It is perhaps time to stop regretting the behaviour of molecular forces.[22]

DeVoto believed that there was no evidence that Samuel Clemens was in any way in conflict with the society of the mining frontier in general. He thrived there. It was there that he found out what he was best fitted for. It was there that Mark Twain and "The Celebrated Jumping Frog" emerged from obscurity. He liked the vigor of the mining camp, all theories notwithstanding. DeVoto described Mark Twain's life in detail. He insisted that Mark Twain knew that "The Celebrated Jumping Frog of Calaveras County" was not great literature. But he also insisted that Brooks misunderstood Mark Twain's statement about the tale. The articles which Mark Twain thought were better were similar in nature to the jumping frog tale; they were examples of the frontier humor that was an integral part of Mark Twain the writer.[23]

## VII   *Mark Twain's Literary Development*

In his final evaluation, DeVoto concluded that it was inevitable that Mark Twain should have developed as he did. His career "epitomized the experience of the West in American history and nothing very much different from what actually happened could have happened." DeVoto believed that the West had shaped political history; but, at the same time, it had absorbed and accepted the education and standards of the East. Mark Twain, a product of the West, accepted these standards; his writing would have been better had he refused the "material and themes of interest to the genteel tradition." Twain's books suffered from the conflict between the two traditions, but he was always a humorist. At the same time, he was too easily influenced by others and had no control over his brilliant imagination.

> He came East and he accepted tuition.—That is a complete description of what happened—as it is an epitome of the western experience. He accepted, to the small extent of which he was capable, with no awareness of any surrender, the dominant criteria of his age.... Much further nonsense could have been avoided if criticism had discovered how little the acceptance of those criteria altered what he was and how little it affected his books. But that would have necessitated reading Mark Twain, whereas criticism has preferred to theorize about him and to read Mr. Brooks.[24]

## VIII   *Mark Twain Criticism*

Chapter IX of *Mark Twain's America,* entitled "The Critics of Mark Twain," is a summary of literary criticism about Mark Twain prior to 1912. The present study, primarily devoted to the most important facet of Twain criticism, the influence of the frontier and frontier humor on Twain's writing, gains little from the chapter. DeVoto noted that in the forty-eight years since the publication of *The Adventures of Huckleberry Finn* no full-length treatment of the book had been done and hoped that the Mark Twain Centennial, three years later, would result in a renewed interest in Mark Twain, as Melville's centennial year had done for him in 1919. After a summary of Mark Twain criticism between 1884 and about 1912, he noted that after that year the bulk of criticism, based on economics and Freud, had emanated from the college professor critics, whom he described as preferring "emotion as opposed to thought, a selective attitude which is hardly different from fanaticism, and a willingness to substitute epithet for analysis in the consideration of what it disapproved. It had also the strength of religion: fervor, the conviction of righteousness, and acquaintance with the resources of rhetoric."[25]

After indicating that the critics had oversimplified the complexity of three centuries of the American heritage, he listed the clichés of the criticism, including the "Frontier, the American, the Puritan, the Pioneer, the Artist, the American Artist, Pioneering Materialism, and Industrial Philistinism." He reiterated the necessity to examine theory in the light of fact, pleaded for rationality, and castigated Brooks's *The Ordeal of Mark Twain*. After summarizing Brooks's position and questioning the amateur Freudian approach, DeVoto wrote: "This is the 'Ordeal' of Mark Twain: that, desiring to be an artist (a rebel against society), he surrendered to the ideals of materialistic America and so betrayed his deepest self. So he suffered throughout his life from a sense of profound guilt, the product of a conflict between art and conformity. What is the mechanism by which he systematically betrayed his destiny? Well, he wrote humor." And then DeVoto added: "Mr. Brooks dislikes humor."[26]

*Mark Twain's America*, in a chapter entitled "The Big Bear of the Arkansaw," described the humor of the frontier better than it had ever been described before, except, perhaps, in Meine's introduction to *Tall Tales of the Southwest*. DeVoto's was a pioneering work; many such studies have since been done. He insisted that, as a "realist writing in the comic tradition, . . . Mark Twain [achieved] his permanence in American literature."[27] Half a paragraph summarized DeVoto's concept of Mark Twain:

> It is enough to assert that he was the culmination of a literature, the expression of humor at its highest level. A frontiersman, a raconteur, a printer and a reporter, his work was shaped by this rendition of the life to which he was native. This humor was his earliest expression and his most constant. Its perceptions and evocations, its methods and materials, its values, its deficiencies, and its weaknesses, were his also. It was the basis of his mind,

as it was the framework of his books. He was always a frontier humorist, who devoted himself to the production of laughter. If he had not been that, he could not have become the satirist and realist who is remembered.[28]

The analysis of *The Adventures of Huckleberry Finn* in the last chapter, "The Artist as American," is, in my opinion, the best of the numerous interpretations of that novel since 1932. An anecdote in the chapter is most revealing of the thinking of Mark Twain and of DeVoto. The February, 1885, issue of *Century Magazine* carried a section from *Huckleberry Finn*, two chapters from Howells' *The Rise of Silas Lapham*, and the first chapters of James's *The Bostonians*. To Mark Twain, Howells' writing seemed "dazzling—masterly—incomparable." As for James, he "would rather be damned to John Bunyan's heaven than read that."[29] The anecdote reveals Mark Twain and explains somewhat the attitude of Brooks and others towards him. Brooks was not the first to ignore the influence and the importance of the American West in American literature. In fact, the influence of Henry James on Brooks seems fairly obvious.

## IX  *Mark Twain Centennial and MLA Speech*

In 1932 DeVoto wrote of the coming celebration of the centennial of Twain's birth in 1935. DeVoto himself was one of the speakers at the concluding exercises of "Mark Twain Week" at the University of Missouri, on December 6, 1935, about three years after the publication of *Mark Twain's America* and about three years before DeVoto became curator of the Mark Twain papers. The speech, which has been reprinted in *Forays and Rebuttals*,[30] obviously was an occasional one; DeVoto's remarks are almost an emotional evangelical sermon. At the same time, the speech is one of the most succinct appraisals of Mark Twain that DeVoto ever made.

After quoting a critic of fifteen years before (the year of Missouri's centennial), one who neither understood nor approved of Mark Twain's writing, DeVoto defended Mark Twain, who by 1935, he said, no longer needed defending. The people had always read Mark Twain, he said, although the critics of the "genteel tradition" were fifty years late in catching up. Making a passing allusion to Brooks's book, which he called the first synthesis in "the new criticism," DeVoto again commented on the critics' obtuseness. He listed as the reasons for such obtuseness those already emphasized in *Mark Twain's America*: the lack of appreciation for humor and a failure to understand frontier America. DeVoto said:

> Mark Twain is nothing accidental. His mother's family crossed the mountains by our oldest gateway, to the limestone and savannas of Kentucky. His father carried this westering to frontier Missouri. And Mark was born in the center of the great valley at the exact moment when the westward nation, hurrying toward empire, leaped from the frontier into the continental void. Step by step, year by year, he accompanied the accelerating empire, a part of that gigantic shaping. Year by year its experience was his, registering in his nerves, piling up the accretions of knowledge in muscle and sinew and bone, while the empire whirled toward climax—and after climax could judge itself, read the registration of the nerves, and determine what, for good or ill but forever, had been changed, gained, or lost.
>
> Small wonder if critics have needed fifty years to understand what happened. As history goes, fifty years is a short time for criticism to lag behind revolutionary art. For, of course, Mark Twain was a revolutionary artist—not in the trivial and transitory meaning now much hymned by dissociated minds, but in the only meaning that literature knows. The bonds and constraints of a national life had been altogether rearranged, and literature had not adjusted itself to the difference. A wedge had been driven between American life and American literature. To drive that wedge out, to bring our literature once more into organic relationship with our national life, to give our life a new, cleared channel in letters—that was the recurrent task of the revolutionary artist.[31]

DeVoto insisted that Mark Twain's greatness was a result of the following facts:

1. He was a frontiersman, a native of Missouri on the fringe of the settlements. The American experience was deeply embodied in him.

2. He had the habits of mind of the frontiersman, including "accuracy of observation and instant and exact application of it."

3. He had the border shrewdness, "the hard-headed realism" caused by a struggle with the wilderness.

4. His humor was the native humor of the frontier.

5. He was the first to write in the vernacular; with him, for the first time, the American language became a "medium of art."

6. He was a satirist of America and of "the damned human race." Some of his satire, DeVoto said, would take its place with that of other immortals—Swift, Rabelais, and Voltaire.

7. He was a myth-maker who rose to universals by "absolute fidelity to the life of his own nation, his own section."

8. Even his minor frontier characters, hundreds of them, were memorably portrayed. These were the population of "the westward making America moving from the frontier through expanding industrialism to empire." He was the first to present this picture.

9. Thus Mark Twain, by picturing these living Americans and by immersing himself in his own people, "came to the universal."

10. He gave a universal picture of the human race; thus he is our contemporary. And thus the critics finally recognized his worth, in a few short years.

After thus explaining Twain's greatness DeVoto made a final evaluation:

> Well, this is the major prophet, the great novelist, the artist as American I declare unto you on his centennial. Recognition of the true greatness of this Missouri frontiersman has had, among the critical, a slow and amazingly obtuse progress. He looks to-day far otherwise, I judge, than he looked to the gentleman whom I quoted when I began to speak. He does not seem a commonplace, coarse, uneducated buffoon, absolutely ignorant of all the canons of literary art. He looks instead like the foremost artist in American literature.[32]

Slightly more than three weeks after his speech in Missouri, on January 1, 1936, DeVoto delivered an address before the American Literature Section of the Modern Language Association at Cincinnati, an article entitled "Mark Twain and the Limits of Criticism."[33] The essay is less an evaluation of Mark Twain than an attack on DeVoto's contemporaries who had written about Twain. He repeated his insistence that to understand Twain one must not be motivated by a political, social, or esthetic bias.[34]

## X  *Curator of the Twain Papers*

DeVoto had just begun writing the "Easy Chair" for *Harper's* and was soon to become, for two years, the editor of the *Saturday Review of Literature,* when in the spring of 1938 the Mark Twain estate appointed him to succeed Paine as custodian of the Mark Twain Papers. DeVoto "arranged them, studied them exhaustively, published some of them as *Mark Twain in Eruption,* and prepared others for publication." He also made the papers available for study by "qualified scholars."[35] In the preface to *Mark Twain at Work,* DeVoto makes a statement that must have given him great satisfaction:

> *Mark Twain's America* was what a later fashion came to call a "social study" of literature. It was grounded, that is, in a belief that a writer's environment is important to his work and that, specifically, much of what was great and fruitful in Mark Twain's books was an expression of a national experience. In view of the reception accorded it in certain quarters, I am happy to say that an exhaustive study of the most intimate Mark Twain papers, published, partly published, and unpublished, has supported every major conclusion of my book. An enlarged edition would not need to revise anything I said in it about Hannibal, the river, the West, or the frontier in general. After four and a half years of work in the Mark Twain Papers I regard my thesis as established.[36]

*Mark Twain at Work* is the last really important criticism of Twain that DeVoto did, with the possible exceptions of a few "Easy Chair" articles. This criticism consists of three essays: "The Symbols of Despair," which according to DeVoto's "acknowledgments," was the William Vaughn Moody Lecture at the University of Chicago, March, 1940; "The Phantasy of Boyhood," the introduction to the scarce Limited Editions Club *Tom Sawyer;* and "Noon and the Dark," the introduction to the Limited Editions Club *Huckleberry Finn.* The introduction to *The Portable Mark Twain,* as one might expect, contains nothing new. DeVoto's interest lay elsewhere; his thesis had been vindicated.

The *Tom Sawyer* essay poetically, in the last paragraph, set forth one attitude towards the frontier:

> As such it [*Tom Sawyer*] perfectly preserves something of the American experience, more of American dreaming, and still more of the beauty that was our heritage and that still conditions both our national memory and our phantasy. On one side of it is Cardiff Hill, a remnant of the great forest, on the other side is the

river: both at the very base of our awareness. Between these beauties the village is sleepy, peaceful, and secure. The world invades it only as romance and adventure; the energies of the age are over the horizon. Time has stopped short; the frontier has passed by and the industrial revolution is not yet born. Life is confident and untroubled, moves serenely at an unhurried pace, fulfills itself in peace. Islanded in security, in natural beauty, St. Petersburg is an idyll of what we once were, of what is now more than ever necessary to remember we once were. Here also the book captures and will keep secure forever a part of America ... of America over the hills and far away.[37]

In setting the time of *Huckleberry Finn,* DeVoto states that it is not later than 1845: "The Mexican War has not occurred, the great migration has not got under way, the mid-continental society does not show the earliest fissures that make its setting toward the Civil War."[38]

DeVoto believed that some minds prefer symbols (like the white whale of *Moby Dick*), while others prefer "experience to metaphysical abstractions and the thing to the symbol." The latter group, he said, think *Huckleberry Finn* is the greatest work of American fiction of the nineteenth century because it is not "a voyage in pursuit of a white whale but a voyage among feudists, mobbers, thieves, rogues, nigger hunters, and murderers, precisely because Huck never encounters a symbol but always some actual human being working out an actual destiny."[39]

DeVoto wrote that Mark Twain himself had been born in the year (1835) when America's greatest social force, westward expansion, had begun to work towards Oregon. He had lived during the 1840's, 1850's and 1860's when the Republic had become the Empire; and he had been a part of the Westward Movement. His secure Western years became his insecure Hartford years; and he also had perceived, for the first time in America, the limitation of the democratic hope. Although *Huckleberry Finn* showed the collision of hope with reality, it is "not a book of despair but rather of realistic acceptance. It accepts democracy not as a journey which will end only at the stars but rather as the terms of arbitration between what is best and what is worst in the damned human race."[40]

DeVoto's work on Mark Twain, besides activating a renewal of interest in Twain's works—an interest that is currently growing—

led DeVoto himself into an area that he continually derided and poked fun at: literary theory and literary criticism. In rising to insist on the use of fact instead of theory in any analysis of Mark Twain, DeVoto found himself in conflict with the critical crowd, both the academics and the scholar-journalists. In order to combat critical theories which he held in contempt, he had to work out theories of his own. He did so, although he continually insisted that the theories should be only relative and should always be subject to revision. But he did, finally, like his contemporaries, put down on paper a literary critical system.

## CHAPTER 3

# The Literary Fallacy: Writer as Critic

## I *DeVoto's Entrance into Criticism*

BERNARD DeVOTO'S entrance into the field of literary theory, most frequently called, then and now, "literary criticism," was, as has been shown, through the back door. He was motivated by his interest in the American frontier and his desire to defend Mark Twain from his detractors. In his speech before the Modern Language Association, DeVoto examined Mark Twain criticism and critical writing in general; he established a basis for objective criticism; but at the same time, like a Missouri mule, he pulled backward, shaking his head, and denied that a basis for objective criticism exists.

A chronological examination of DeVoto's books reveals a consistent pattern of development in his thinking. A similar examination of DeVoto's magazine articles reveals a comparable pattern: he gradually was developing a critical stance. Almost from the beginning of his career, DeVoto's magazine articles showed a wide range of interests, but the frontier ideal and its impact on American institutions was the most apparent and most frequent theme.

A large number of the serious articles written between 1931 and 1936, many of them about the American West, were published in 1936 in *Forays and Rebuttals*. About these articles DeVoto wrote: "I had thought of my contributions to the 'quality group' as occasional interruptions of more serious or more frivolous occupations, always instigated by some editor, usually Lee Hartman, who knew my inability to say no and managed to make his request when I could not possibly afford the time to comply with it." But, DeVoto wrote, in restrospect he found that he had contributed to the "quality group" more than he had expected; in fact, he was practically a staff writer for *Harper's* even before he took over the "Easy Chair."[1]

Not very much of the critical material appeared in *Forays and Rebuttals*. An exception was an essay reprinted from *Harper's* (January, 1934), entitled "How Not to Write History," in which DeVoto made a biting comment on the methods of the literary critic. For many years, he wrote, the search for the American mind and similar personifications called "the American point of view," "the soul of America," and "the American experience" was limited to politicians, evangelical clergymen, and foreigners (especially Englishmen on tour). But in about 1914, a number of literary critics, having read a few American novels and essays, began to rewrite history. Their apprenticeship had been in literary criticism, "a profession in which impreciseness of idea is a virtue and a generalized sentiment is much better than a fact." The result was "interpretation"—a search for symbols which could be personified. These people—evidently those who had begun to use the words "pioneer," "frontier," and "the West" in ways to which DeVoto objected—were ignorant of history. For history they substituted what they called "higher truths": poetic perceptions, guesses, and beautiful notions. He wrote, "Ignorance is not a satisfactory equipment for a historian, and it is not helped much by a disdain of the methods and materials of history."[2]

Also, in *Forays and Rebuttals*, in an essay on the methods of Lytton Strachey as a biographer, reprinted from *Harper's* (January, 1933), DeVoto wrote, "For a while he [Strachey] wrote literary criticism, an activity in which uncontrolled speculation is virtuous and responsibility is almost impossible."[3] But DeVoto was still writing articles, mainly about the West, and grumbling about the critics of Mark Twain. The last two essays in *Forays and Rebuttals* were the Mark Twain speeches.

In the years between 1936 and 1940, when *Minority Report* was published, DeVoto was drawn more and more into literary controversy. Many of the articles he wrote for the quality magazines were reprinted in *Minority Report*, and DeVoto began his attacks on the literary critics of the 1920's and, not quite as directly, on the writers of the Lost Generation. The DeVoto who firmly eschewed literary dicta had begun, protesting all the while, to pontificate about literature. In March, 1943, he made a series of lectures at Indiana University, published in 1944 as *The Literary Fallacy*. Still insisting that literary criticism was an impossibility, DeVoto himself proposed standards that were the same as those he had demanded in *Mark Twain's America*. *The Literary Fallacy* is typically energetic and meaty, and the controversy deserves more consideration than it can be given here. A central aspect of the controversy—varying attitudes towards American civilization—will be discussed later.

Then, in 1950, DeVoto published *The World of Fiction*, which, despite the author's insistence that the work was neither esthetics nor literary criticism, is entirely literary theory. DeVoto's description—the book is merely "an analysis of the relationship between the person who writes a novel and the person who reads it"—proclaims it as such; and it is probably DeVoto's weakest and most popular critical work. In the preface DeVoto admitted that the things he had to say were obvious, but he maintained that they were so obvious that it was time that someone said them.[4]

## II  *MLA Speech*

The most important document in the establishment of the direction of DeVoto's literary theory was to take was his Modern Language Association speech of January 1, 1936: "Mark Twain and the Limits of Criticism." It was essentially an attack on those literary critics who DeVoto felt had written without using the facts. DeVoto's intention in the speech was to examine Mark Twain's books and some of the books written about him, in order to establish "errors of fact, contradictions of principle and fallacies of reasoning" and to reveal "more or less fundamental dilemmas or paradoxes in the critical process."[5] Moreover, DeVoto set up in the speech criteria to be used in critical judgment, criteria which he developed further in *The Literary Fallacy;* he also stated his prejudices and assumptions which, he believed, were likely to influence his views:

First, he believed that criticism is necessarily "an imprecise method of studying literature." Second, the critic cannot be unequivocal or objective. Third, the methods and results of criticism are limited by the "preconceptions and unconscious trends" of the critics. Fourth, "critical generalizations are never completely applicable to literature." Fifth, critical systems, "however learned, logical and exhaustive, and however valuable as social or intellectual documents," have only a secondary importance for literature because of the essential nature of the creative process and because the emotions and intellect of the critic separates him from the material which he criticizes. DeVoto said, "I accept the extension of these beliefs to the essay I am reading."[6]

Several kinds of criticism were then discussed and discarded by DeVoto. They were (1) the study of vocabulary, which, he said, was interesting but had no value except as "an acceptable answer to the ever-present problem of what to do with the candidate for the M.A. in literature"; (2) the study of texts, which is of doubtful value because one deals with finished works of art: "criticism must necessarily deal with the version of *Huckleberry Finn* that was given to us"; (3) the study of influences, which can be important so long as the critic limits himself to "an effort to determine the total cultural possession of the literary artist, his liaisons with his time and the civilization of which he is a part"; and (4) theoretical, systematic criticism, wherein a "logically unified system of criteria are set up" and the works of a writer are judged by them.

The fourth system, DeVoto said, is inadequate because (1) here criticism usurps a function of literature, (2) it is likely to distort the literature it criticizes, (3) it assumes that there are "right and wrong ways of writing books," (4) it tries "to reduce a writer to a single meaning, on which it may pass judgment," (5) it tells more about the critic than it does about the writer, and (6) the critic begins with a theory, his own experience projected in a theory, and then sets out in search for proof.[7]

In his comment on the value of the study of influences, a part of which is given above, DeVoto had much to say, because it was on this point that he had violently differed with Van Wyck Brooks four years before. The most pertinent paragraphs follow:

> Let me say at once that this activity may exist on two planes, and that on one of them criticism performs one of its most important services. So far as the study of influence is an effort to determine the total cultural possession of a literary artist, his liaisons with his time and the civilization of which he is a part, just that far it is the most valuable branch of literary studies. It is certain to be incomplete always, wrong more often than it is right, grotesquely wrong a good part of the time, and right chiefly in

flashes of inspiration and by the grace of God. Nevertheless it gives us dependable information and ideas, and it establishes a skeleton and outline on which to base ethical, social and esthetic judgments by which we record and may even assay our own culture.

But the study of influences does not always or even often exist on that plane. More often it attempts to erect bit by bit a foundation on which, presumably, others may build the edifice. And this humble effort turns into a hunt for sources. The study of literary influences is mostly uncontrollable by fact, and almost always the search for specific sources of works of the imagination is usually evidence that the person who engages in it does not understand the creative process. He is disqualified by ignorance of esthetics and particularly the psychology of esthetics. He is disqualified by ignorance of general and individual psychology. And he is deficient both in practical experience and in the associative functions of intelligence that qualify one to understand literature.[8]

To the statement by Wagenknecht that *The Adventures of Tom Sawyer* was strongly influenced by *Don Quixote,* DeVoto said, "Nonsense." *Tom Sawyer,* he said, is a great book because "as we at once recognize from our own experience, it is shaped by life—not because it is influenced by Cervantes." Then he said,

When Dr. Brashear describes to me a Hannibal so cultured, so acquainted with literary tradition that, it seems, the natives acted first from the library and only secondarily from the appetites and passions of life, when she presents Mark Twain to me as a writer accepted in the thought and feeling of eighteenth-century literature I can only say, this is the process that has made a literary dictaphone of Poe, and it is wrong. Let us appeal to experience and to Mark Twain's books. I do not doubt that the western town where I was ten years old in 1907 contained fifty copies of Xenophon's *Anabasis,* for there were at least fifty people who could have carried them there from school—as Miss Brashear has found a great many eighteenth-century classics in Missouri private libraries where Mark Twain was ten. Yet fifty Xenophons do not make my home town a cultured society deeply embued with the Greek spirit. It was in fact a crude, coarse, ignorant and even illiterate society, for all its libraries. I did not read the *Anabasis* till I was thirty-five, and though my father's library contained a copy of the *Noctes Ambrosianae,* it remains to me and in my library a set of four books into which I have never looked, and would remain that though a hundred sets were found in Utah between 1905 and 1915. Are Mark Twain's books full of wit, "characters," discursive essays, and formally developed satirical sketches on human folly? So are many books of his own time and every other time. Those are not indexes of an eighteenth-century inheritance, they are the common and perennial modes of literature. And, *in fact,* is the Hannibal which exists in Mark's books a focus of eighteenth-century culture? Are, in fact, the emotions, sentiments and patterns in them eighteenth-century? The whole force of intelligence is that they are not—that they issue directly and concretely from their time and place, a frontier Missouri settlement before the Civil War where a new, native way of life was in process of formation, a way of life that had as little in common with the eighteenth century as with the eighth. In short, Mark Twain was a literary artist employing his fantasy on the immediate material of experience.[9]

Thus DeVoto insisted that literature is created by the force exerted by the entire external world surrounding the writer on the writer's "organic emotional life," and that this force is beyond the reach of influence or of critical analysis.[10] And he insisted that human experience is "almost exclusively the source of all creative writing."[11]

As examples of those who approached Twain to prove their prepossessions, DeVoto cited Vernon Louis Parrington, whose "prepossessions . . . require him to bring all things into judgment by means of Thomas Jefferson's libertarian commonwealth"; Ludwig Lewisohn, whose several systems include rejection of all that he dislikes in American life, such as sexual repression and the Protestant sects, and admiration of the German or Jewish culture; and who categorized Twain merely as a "folk artist"; Van Wyck Brooks, who intended to study Twain in relation to American life but merely denounced American life; Calverton, who believed that "the petty bourgeois ideology of the frontier" explains Mark Twain; and Granville Hicks, whose conclusions were "tentative and inconclusive" about Mark Twain, mainly, DeVoto thought, because Hicks knew Twain's work better than did the others and because of the publication of *Mark Twain's America* ("a book which appeared a year or two before *The Great Tradition*"). DeVoto's conclusions were "that knowledge of an author's work and respect for fact are deterrents to systematic criticism."[12]

DeVoto concluded his "intolerably long" paper with the following comments:

> Now consider this. Mr. Parrington, Mr. Brooks, Mr. Lewisohn and Mr. Calverton have all brought Mark Twain to the judgment bar of different critical systems. Add the genteel critics and the humanists, whom I have not had time to examine here. Add my own suggestively systematized attempt to avoid systematic criticism. Here we have seven different systems. They give us seven diffrent sets of findings. Each one of them presents a different Mark Twain, and asks us to accept him, forsaking all others. The seven Mark Twains thus derived are mutually contradictory. The inhibited artist of Mr. Brooks contradicts the freely functioning folk-artist of Mr. Lewisohn. The petty bourgeois of Mr. Calverton is incompatible with Mr. Parrington's Jeffersonian and socialist. Any one of them obliterates all the others. Yet all seven systems are applied to the analysis of the same body of facts, the books which Mark Twain wrote, which are available in the Household Edition, and which remain unchanged.
>
> I conclude that Mark Twain's books are something apart from and independent of the criticism that seven different systems have applied to them. I conclude that criticism has found no way of representing literature that is divorced from the critic's temperament, no way, that is, of compelling a skeptic's acceptance. I conclude that these seven systems are arbitrary and subjective.[13]

Then DeVoto, despite his "suggestively systematized attempts to avoid systematic criticism," finally suggested two useful fields of criticism:

> It seems to me that the most fruitful fields of criticism are esthetics and social history. Esthetic criticism is flagrantly and frankly subjective, and experiences a cyclical shift of fashions similar to the one I have pointed out in systematic criticism. The despair of such a critic as Mr. Krutch or Mr. Richards proceeds from no unwillingness to accept its comparatives and an attempt to ground them on an absolute in psychology or revelation. Mr. T. S. Eliot struggled with the same dilemma until esthetic revelation merged with theological revelation and made him a systematic critic. So long as esthetics frankly accepts the relativity of its results, however, it avoids the morass and remains indispensable to the study of literature. It is the immediate nexus between literature and the student. It is furthermore, a record of taste and so an index to and vehicle of the culture of any given period.

Social history treats esthetic criticsm and systematic criticism as objective facts and uses them as points of orientation in its descriptive study. Its opportunity for analysis, however, is in the fourth field of inquiry that I described some pages back, the study of what a writer was understood to mean by a given class at a given time. To determine what a writer "meant" in his work as a whole is clearly a subjective undertaking. But what a writer meant at any given time to any clearly defined group of people is an objective fact and can be determined with some objectivity. Such an inquiry seems to me not only the most meaningful but also the most important occupation of literary criticism. By pursuing it criticism can reveal significant facts and linkages of facts in culture and civilization and can escape the subjective whirlpools that make certain of its other inquiries so nearly impotent.[14]

## III    DeVoto, Literary Theorist

Thus DeVoto constantly insisted that the literary critic must strive for objectivity; with equal vigor he asserted that for the most part such objectivity is impossible, and that the critical theorist must admit the subjectivity and changeability of esthetic criticism and must be content with this ambivalence. By 1936 DeVoto had begun to be a literary theorist, although he vociferously objected to being considered one.

*Minority Report* contains more of DeVoto's attack on Van Wyck Brooks and the "Young Intellectuals" of the 1920's. In an essay first printed in the *Saturday Review of Literature,* September 26, 1936—the first issue of the magazine with DeVoto as editor—he flailed away at those who wanted to create a real civilization in America while there was yet time. ("Since 1912," DeVoto wrote, "it has always been 11:59 in America, and only a few heroic literary folk to fend doom away.") And what was the equipment of those young men? he asked. They were, he wrote, "characterized by a stupefying ignorance of what they were talking about, an instinctive fear of experience, and a vocational preference for describing America by gazing into the crystals of their souls. They knew no history. The American frontier was where Rousseau's disciples went; down to the Civil War American life was a simple unity of homogeneous people; the nation had never produced a reformer or a rebel; . . ."[15]

Their ignorance of history, of the facts of the Westward Movement, was DeVoto's main charge against the critics of the 1920's.

The second charge against them was their following the leadership of Van Wyck Brooks, who did not understand the significance of the frontier. DeVoto wrote,

> The generation's finest critic was Mr. Van Wyck Brooks. He most brilliantly of all set out to find a usable past, most bitterly discovered that there was none, and most logically and rigorously worked out the generation's master idea, that American life stifled moral courage and spiritual greatness and true art. And lately Mr. Brooks has published a wise, profound, and very moving book in which he finds a usable past and turns up in the craven America the most astonishing courage in letters and leadership, the most amazing spiritual endeavor in the literary life, and the most astounding excellence of art in the wine of the Puritans. If one makes parallel columns of quotations from *The Flowering of New England* and from the books which Mr. Brooks was writing fifteen and twenty years ago, one beholds the best of the generation making a formal recantation.[16]

DeVoto felt a sadness about the Younger Generation, which seems in part to be the critical counterpart of the Lost Generation:

> And so by 1936 the generation has arrived at the position from which Robert Frost started in 1913.
>
> A vigorous and colorful generation, an emancipated and emancipating generation, the most interesting generation of our literature. But a wishful generation, impermeable to experience, separated by iridescent mist from the realities of men and women living on this continent, conjuring up an America of phantasy and out of theory, syllogisms, and boyhood lacks. And too soft. Times were easy, success and reputation were too easily come by, it was too much respected and too gently handled by itself, by its critics, and specially by the public.[17]

## IV  *DeVoto and Wilson*

Edmund Wilson, in the February 3, 1937, issue of *New Republic*, wrote a critical essay in which he took DeVoto to task for taking Van Wyck Brooks to task. In general the article is a strong attack on *Mark Twain's America*, which Mr. Wilson had read none too carefully. He said, for instance, that DeVoto deplored frontier humor—a statement that is about as far away from an understanding of the book as one could get. Wilson complimented DeVoto for giving new life to book reviewing, for insisting on responsible criticism. None too kindly, however, he wrote,

> Yet precisely because Mr. DeVoto has undertaken this kind of responsible criticism, we expect more of him than he has given us. We expect of him an intelligible basis of taste and an intelligible point of view. He *sounds* as if he were being discriminating in his discussion of the relative merits of books, yet the standards by which he judges them remains obscure; he *sounds* as if his strictures on other people's doctrines were based on some deeply thought out philosophy of which he was very sure, yet though we keep on reading him in the interested expectation of finding out what that philosophy is, the revelation never breaks. He is positive and plainspoken on the surface, but when we try to go below the surface, we find ideas that seem erratic and confused.[18]

DeVoto answered the article in the February 13, 1937, issue of the *Saturday Review of Literature*. Later he expanded the answer into a chapter in *Minority Report* entitled "Autobiography: or, As Some Call It, Literary Criticism." In answer to Wilson's question as to what he stood for, DeVoto wrote that he distrusted absolutes and opposed them. "And with them," he wrote, "let me include prophecy, simplification, generalization, abstract logic, and especially the habit of mind which consults theory first and experience only afterward." Furthermore,

> I am, if you must have words, a pluralist, a relativist, an empiricist. I am at home with the concrete inquiries of historians and scientists, and uneasy among the abstractions of critics and metaphysicians. I confine myself to limited questions; I try to use methods that can be controlled by fact and experience; I am unwilling to let enthusiasm or desire or a vision of better things carry me farther than the methods will go by themselves. I rest ultimately on experience and, where that fails, on common sense. No one need tell me how incomplete and imperfect they are, how misinterpretation and falsification betray them, how tentative, fragile, and unsatisfactory the conclusions we base them on must be. I know: but they are more dependable than anything else. They are, especially, more dependable than gospels.[19]

## V  The Literary Fallacy

In the Pattern Lectures at the University of Indiana in March, 1943, DeVoto's final evaluation of the critics of the 1920's was made. He revised the first lecture, added new material, and divided it into two chapters. The lectures were published in April, 1944, as *The Literary Fallacy.*

Again it is difficult to assess *The Literary Fallacy* without doing a detailed study of the critics whom he criticized—and such a study should be done. Standing alone, however, the book is both readable and interesting. In it DeVoto stated clearly what he believed to be the shortcomings of the literary critics. His conclusions were based on the ideas which he had consistently held throughout the Mark Twain controversy: that a writer must be examined in the context of the environment which produced him and that any conclusions the critic draws must also be based on the *facts*—the facts of background and of the work itself.

His belief that the text itself must be studied agrees with the views of Cleanth Brooks and Robert Penn Warren, whose ideas were beginning to infiltrate the college English classes of the late 1930's and early 1940's, although in the more conservative schools *Understanding Poetry* was sometimes read surreptitiously by the students. But DeVoto's belief in the need for careful study of the author's background did not agree completely with the early Brooks and Warren, and not at all with the criticism of the "Chicago School," which ignored biography and history.

In *The Literary Fallacy* DeVoto denied any intent of doing a full survey of the literature and criticism of the 1920's; yet he conceded that reviewers of the book would probably ignore his denial (and the reader might wish that he had done the full survey). DeVoto described the book:

> . . . It is an examination, reasonably complete but far from complete, of certain ideas, dogmas, and conclusions which appear and reappear in much American literature of the 1920's, particularly in the work of writers who were then widely held to be most characteristic of the time and most expressive of its spirit. Whatever their context, they are literary ideas, dogmas, and conclusions. Sometimes they appear in considerable purity and intensity, as principal or even exclusive themes. Sometimes they are mixed, weak, or tangential. Sometimes they appear as assumptions or prepossessions rather than theses, or as reflection of the theses of others, or as tones or overtones of belief rather than formulated opinions. Sometimes they color a writer's work only a little. Sometimes they appear in the books of the same writer, or

even in the same book, with varying degrees of intensity. My purpose is to examine various appearances of these ideas, dogmas, and conclusions, to appraise their validity, and to study some of the relationships among them.[20]

This phenomenon which DeVoto examined in detail he called "the literary fallacy," which consisted of a series of fallacies in logic, "defects in observation and understanding," and "errors in fact." He was going to analyze the entire complex literary situation and draw conclusions from the analysis.[21]

The writers of the 1920's thought in patterns that caused them to draw erroneous conclusions, DeVoto believed. There were good writers during that decade, lively, vigorous, and entertaining; but they were ignored by those who attempted to "enforce a test oath on writers . . . to impose on literature stated imperatives and fixed orthodoxy." Defenders of the literature of the 1920's insisted that the literature merely reflected a confused, anarchic, sick society. The truth was, DeVoto insisted, that the literature of the 1920's repudiated American life and shut itself away from the realities of that life. The best-known writers, such as H. L. Mencken, Sinclair Lewis, Ernest Hemingway, John Dos Passos, William Faulkner, and Thomas Wolfe, did not picture American life in the 1920's as it really was.[22]

## VI  *Literary Inbreeding and Brooks's Influence*

Archibald MacLeish, in 1940, in a book called *The Irresponsibles*, insisted that the irresponsibility of modern writers consisted of their careful describing of things as they were. But, to DeVoto, the basic error of contemporary writers was that they did *not* report objectively the nature of American life. In 1941 Van Wyck Brooks (and DeVoto agreed with him) insisted that modern writers had lost contact with American life and with the American people. They were inbred; they poisoned one another and society with their despair. The irony, DeVoto added, lay in the fact that Van Wyck Brooks was "truly an active agent in shaping the literature of the 1920's," because others had followed his lead and built their theses on his. In 1941 Brooks sought to reject the ideas that had stemmed from his own.[23]

DeVoto repeated the charge that in the beginning Brooks sought to judge America by its literature and nothing else; moreover, he ignored such vital figures as Melville and E. A. Robinson and only casually mentioned London, Norris, and Dreiser. Also, he ignored the literature of the Great Valley and even the lesser-known "rich New England literature which exists apart from the classics." Brooks's facts were weak, but he made sweeping generalizations about American institutions. Sometimes he made subjective statements not based on any facts whatsoever. Other writers followed him, and the literary fallacy came into full bloom.[24]

This method of criticism DeVoto condemned:

> In some departments of intellectual life this would be an extremely serious accusation. One must understand at the very beginning, however, that it is not a serious or even a relevant accusation according to the way of thinking which these lectures examine. In that way of thinking the criterion of an idea is its rightness as idea, not the knowledge which it represents or its correspondence to reality. The method of literary thinking proceeds from idea to idea by way of idea, with no check or control outside idea. It deduces ideas from assumptions, general principles, and universal abstract truths. It requires facts to conform to logic and it ascertains facts by determining what logic implies.[25]

DeVoto's criticisms of this method include the following: (1) Brooks was ignorant of biography. (2) He refused to face the social implications of slavery, developing industrialism, and westward expansion: "One is required to know that the Mexican War involved all three and brought the first and third to climax." (3) Mr. Brooks confused "the social issue" with "the literary issue." (4) His description of American life seldom touched reality. America, he thought, was "provincial, bougeois (in the Flaubertian, not the Marxian sense), and therefore hostile to men of talent. We are therefore a business civilization." (5) Mr. Brooks equated Calvinism and Puritanism and with that term gave the 1920's "their supreme eidolon, and he holds it responsible for all our offenses." (6) Mr. Brooks believed that writers have a three-fold function: to serve as a standard of culture, to pass judgments on society, and to lead society. (7) Mr. Brooks wanted writers to be an Academy which would have "final jurisdiction over esthetic matters and questions of taste." (8) American society has never granted such authority to literary men; and for this reason Brooks did not like American society. (9) Mr. Brooks's criteria for literature were European, not American, and he censured American literature for not being the *same* as European literature. "And with that censure," DeVoto wrote, "the theoretical structure of his first period is completed."[26]

DeVoto then analyzed Brooks's later critical ideas:

> His criticism is now seen to be abstract, deductive, contradictory, unsupported by fact, not derived either from the literature or the society it discusses, and what logicians call argument in a circle. There are no great American writers because American society is not great, and the proof is that it has produced no great writers. The central failure of our writers comes from their flaccid willingness merely to express our culture, but their central failure is a result of their being cut off from our culture. Our greatest need is to develop a native literature which shall express our native life, but on the other hand, we have no native life, and on the other hand writers who express our native life growing from native roots are at fault for not having produced a literature like that of England, France, or Russia.[27]

Brooks, DeVoto insisted, had failed to make contact with reality. He felt that America had to be saved by writers from its barren culture based on acquisitiveness. So Brooks was to lead a movement which would provide that new literature and fruitful national life. DeVoto agreed that these ideas were hopeful, passionately felt, and generous and that they expressed "a fierce idealism which desires to keep America faithful to its promise"; but he also felt that the ideas were doomed because of Brooks's ignorance of the American past and American literature. DeVoto said that he read Brooks's theories "constantly agape at his ... falsification." He said that Brooks, by his own admission, first wrote and then read the literature he had written about.

But, DeVoto thought, the most hopeless error was "not ignorance but the method of approach." Then he defined what he believed to be the basis of the entire literary movement as he wrote about the method of the critics of the 1920's:

> That method is the method of abstract, deductive reasoning, anchored not in objective and verifiable realities but in general principles, proceeding under no factual control, out of purely theoretical observations, to purely theoretical conclusions. It is a complex organization of prepossessions, assumptions, arguments, errors and emotions—a dynamism which I have here chosen to call the literary fallacy.

Reduced to general terms, the literary fallacy assumes: that a culture may be understood and judged solely by means of its literature, and that literature embodies truly and completely both the values and the content of a culture, that literature is the measure of life, and finally that life is subordinate to literature.[28]

DeVoto, in a note to Chapter II, said that he was hesitant to attack Brooks again, since he had already made one attack on him. After reviewing the literature, however, he had found that he "could not find anyone else whose ideas were as intelligent, integrated, central, and influential as his. He was not only the leader of the movement, he was its best mind." In another note DeVoto summarized the reasons for his attack on the criticism of the 1920's:

There is a curious continuity in Mr. Brooks, a central ignorance or a central misunderstanding, which is common to the entire movement. He repeatedly attacks the very thing which he also says America lacked altogether; he specifically laments the absence of things which he rebukes us for having. He, with his entire school, failed to see that the establishment on this continent of new hopes and opportunities and ways of life, the enhancement of human expectation, the democratization of society, the development of democratic government, the expansion of the frontier, the adventure of opening and occupying a continent, the adaptation of Europeans to novel conditions of life which produced "the American, this new man," the evolution of a native culture, the accretion of an American society—he failed to see that such things were in fact what he reproached us for not having, a national fabric of spiritual experience. Our spiritual experience was different from Europe's—that was the fact behind his perception. But from that perception followed two findings: that therefore it was an inferior spiritual experience, and that therefore we had no spiritual experience at all. From that point on his system, or the system of his followers, could use either finding as the occasion might require. That simple logical process produced much harmless nonsense and much dangerous nonsense in the literature of the 1920's.[29]

DeVoto admitted that Brooks's *The Flowering of New England* (1936) and *New England: Indian Summer* (1940) corrected to a great degree many statements about American life and literature which he had earlier made. These books, according to DeVoto, had been based on a reading of the literature; Brooks had begun to base his books on facts and not upon theories. But the harm had been done; too many other authors had followed in his footsteps.

Moreover, Brooks had completely ignored the Civil War because he had not been "able to reduce it to a literary movement." And Brooks's books were still limited by the literary fallacy since he still wrote too much about literature and too little about real life. In writing about New England, Brooks also did not take into account "the life of the people beyond the frontiers of Canaan."[30] DeVoto believed that Brooks's works about New England emphasized the minor writers and the frustrated major writers. He brilliantly pictured the second-rate Holmes and praised Howells, and his essay on James was "the best study of the book [*The Flowering of New England*]." The reason was that James's frustration was "primarily a literary frustration."

On the other hand, DeVoto wrote, Brooks could not understand the source of Henry Adams's frustration: "Adams's failure to be in touch with America." Other writers whom Brooks misunderstood were Emily Dickinson, Longfellow, Lowell, Emerson, Whittier, and Parkman, all for the same reason: Brooks's basic misunderstanding of the facts of American history and American life. DeVoto concluded that others, including T. S. Eliot, followed in Brooks's footsteps and eventually began to study fragments of works instead of whole works. Criticism became "the criticism of the criticism of the criticism." In 1915 the critics had set out to explain the sterility of American culture; but, by 1943, criticism itself had become culturally sterile.

DeVoto described how it got that way: "The answer is simple. If literary criticism has achieved paralysis, it got there by following strictly literary paths, by applying its own conceptions in accordance with its own methods. If it ends self-supported in pure air, unattached to American experience or any other experience, the end follows inevitably from the beginning. The effort to appraise a culture by means of purely literary criteria had no possible outcome except failure."[31]

### VII  *Failures of the Critics of the 1920's*

In Chapter IV of *The Literary Fallacy*, entitled "Waste Land," DeVoto developed his thesis that the writers of the 1920's were too far removed from the reality of American experience, that they were too dependent upon each other, that a sort of literary inbreeding had taken place with monstrous results. He listed and discussed Edgar Lee Masters, Sinclair Lewis, Hemingway, T. S. Eliot, Dos Passos, Faulkner, and Ezra Pound. He believed that second-rate writers (and he seemed to include James T. Farrell in this group) were less susceptible to the literary fallacy than their more noted contemporaries. And he listed as first-rate writers who "stood outside the movement" Carl Sandburg, E. A. Robinson, Willa Cather, Stephen Vincent Benét, and Robert Frost.

He concluded that Frost and the others who had not lost touch with reality had asserted that human feeling and experience do have dignity. The "orthodox" literary figures did not acknowledge this fact. Really, DeVoto wrote, the orthodox writers of America did not approve of democracy and either ignored it or opposed it. They did not accept the humanistic belief "that man is entitled to primary respect because only in man's consciousness can the universe be grappled with" or the democratic belief "that the dignity of man is unalienable."[32]

## VIII   The American Frontiers

In Chapter V, "The Artificers," DeVoto listed examples of two vital areas of which the writers and critics of the 1920's seemed to be ignorant: the American Western frontier and the new frontiers of science. As examples of the first, he cited the work of three government bureaus—the Geological Survey, the Bureau of Ethnology, and the Reclamation Service—and discussed at length the work of men involved in the frontier experience, especially Clarence King, friend of Henry Adams, and John Wesley Powell, one-armed explorer of the Green and Colorado rivers. Powell, he wrote, knew more about what it would take to settle the West and to develop the American democratic system than any other man. His writing, including his *Report on the Lands of the Arid Regions of the United States*, was of great importance; yet none of the critics of the 1920's had heard of Powell.

In a summary which parallels ideas found in Walter Prescott Webb's *The Great Plains* (Webb also was a great admirer of

Powell), DeVoto showed how American institutions changed when the Great Plains were encountered and how (he was to develop this thesis later) the federal government alone could develop some of the Western areas. To DeVoto, "The dedicated literary intelligence of our time ventured to pass judgment on American life without taking into account such men as Powell and such institutions as the Geological Survey. The literary intelligence did not know that such men and such institutions existed. Its judgments were ignorant. They were also arrogantly naive, dilettante, arty, and a little epicene. Who licensed literary men to be ignorant of the things they presumed to judge?"[33]

DeVoto also discussed briefly the medical achievements of the 1920's, especially the increasing knowledge about the treatment of burns, as a facet of the conquest of ignorance. DeVoto, although he did not make such an assertion specifically, seemed to be saying that geographical frontiers and the frontiers of science are the vital influences on American civilization and have always been. The American writer must be conscious of these forces. He seemed to place importance on regional American literature, although to insist on its importance would be to declare the importance of his own belletristic works.

Thus DeVoto's main complaint against the writers of the decade following World War I was that they were ignorant of that which they criticized—American culture:

> We have thus come back to a familiar fact: the repudiation of American life by American literature during the 1920's signified that writers were isolated or insulated from the common culture. There is something intrinsically absurd in the image of a literary man informing a hundred and twenty million people that their ideals are base, their beliefs unworthy, their ideas vulgar, their institutions corrupt, and, in sum, their civilization too trivial to engage the literary man's respect. That absurdity is arrogant but also it is naive and most of all it is ignorant. For the repudiation was the end-product of systems of thinking, and the systems arose in an ignorance that extended to practically everything but imaginative literature and critical comment on it. Systematic critics, that is, worked heroically in the books of the novelists, poets, and one another and disregarded nearly everything else. No doubt in one light they exhibit an exalted devotion to pure thought, but in another light they exhibit the odd spectacle of the literary intelligence committing suicide.[34]

## IX  DeVoto's Credo

Then in the last chapter, "The Meal in the Firkin," DeVoto drew his conclusions, again based on the thesis that in order to write well about America one must first know America. He discussed the settlement of the West and the end of the frontier when, he wrote, "our oldest tradition, our most powerful force, had, technically, reached its end." He discussed immigration, urbanization, and the development of big business. He discussed the development of sections such as the South and the Middle West, the growing complexities of American civilization, and the growth and simultaneous complexity of individual freedom. The world that the critics found drab and lifeless, he wrote, was actually the most cheerful and energetic society in the world. America was not uniform but was variegated and diverse. But still, according to Edmund Wilson, writers in American continually attacked the culture which produced them. And, DeVoto insisted, never in any culture or age had they been so wrong. The literature, in general, was trivial and despairing. Nobody wrote with the authority of an Emerson or a Mark Twain. Both of these men had rebuked their contemporaries, but "both spoke with authority to a people who acknowledged their authority—because both spoke knowing whereof they spoke, and both spoke from within."

DeVoto believed that World War II was changing the attitude of writers toward America, but he did not express any great hope for improvement. He did not believe that "ignorant love is more stable than ignorant contempt." At the end of the last address made to Indiana University students during World War II (and the end of the last chapter of *The Literary Fallacy*), Bernard DeVoto came as near as he ever did to prescribing exactly how books ought to be written. The passage is emotional in its tone, evangelistic in its fervor, and vivid in its diction:

> But, a literary man, I too can succumb to the persuasiveness of literary ideas—I can tell you a moral which the writers of my time have pointed for the writers of your time. I can tell you what literature will have to do if it is to be what, in the faraway, expectant dawn of my era, it set out to be.
>
> If literature is to be a dependable description of America, if it is to make a useful comment on America, then first of all it must

know America. The word "ignorance" has had to run through these lectures like a leitmotif. For the guesses, phantasies, and deductions which contented so many of the writers we have talked about, it must substitute patient years—years of study, years of experience. Knowledge is a slow growth, a long path beset with possibilities of error. Men are not given to know the nature of things by intuition. Authority is not born full-grown in any mind, nor can anyone come to it by staring into his own soul, or at his navel, or into the high priest's emerald breastplate. No one can know a country or a people, no one can know even the small portions with which most of us must be content, except by a long effort to know them, a refusal to be satisfied with the nobly vague, a distrust of the logically beautiful. Knowledge does not come from the matching up of myths, abstractions, and hypotheses that made the writers of the 1920's sure they were red to the shoulders with the blood of life when they were only watching the play of shadows across the screen of their own souls. Knowledge means sweat and doggedness, a realization that one can never know enough, and it comes from experience inappeasably sought after and tested with the most powerful reagents the mind can use. Writers must be content to hold their peace until they know what they are talking about. Readers must be willing to hold them to the job if they refuse to hold themselves. An uninstructed gentleness toward writers has been the mistake of readers in our time. Words like "fool" and "liar" might profitably come back to use. If literature is a trivial pursuit, folly and lying are of no particular moment, but if literature is to be serious then it cannot be permitted folly and lying and when they appear in it they must be labeled and denounced.

Yet knowledge can be come by. But first there is a fixed barrier which writers cannot cross except by virtue of a profound humility. The moral of our literature between the wars is that literature must come upon futility and despair unless it begins in fellowship from within. Rejection, the attitude of superiority, disdain of the experience of ordinary people, repudiation of the values to which the generality of a writer's countrymen devote their lives—the literature of my generation tried that path and found that the path ended in impotence and the courtship of death. The evils and abuses of society may be intolerable but my generation has proved that literature can do nothing whatever about them from outside. It must enter in, it must speak its "Thou shalt!" as one who shares the dust and thirst. Cut the umbilical cord and what dies is not society but literature. Form coteries of the initiate, turn in abhorrence from the village square to the High Place, consecrate yourself to anything which the louts at the foot of the High Place cannot know, however fine or noble or beautiful it may be—and in the end you have only a group of the merely literary, speaking fretfully to one another in soft voices while the tides of the world sweep by.

Either literature deals honestly with the basic experiences in which all men may see themselves, or else it is only a mannered diversion practised by the impaired and of interest only to the leisure moments of those who are whole. Either it is a man and a brother speaking to men and brothers, speaking of the things which all share and are subject to, or else it is only a private titillation. Well over a century ago Ralph Waldo Emerson ordered the American writer to his job—to the meal in the firkin, the milk in the pan. To know what it was that had appeared upon the earth, this new man, this American. To search his heart, his mind, his vision, his memory. Only in obeying that command has American literature ever found reality. Our literature can be true only as it is true of us, it can be great only as it comes to find greatness. All roots will be winterkilled and all the sweet green shoots will die except as they are warmed and fertilized by the common experience of Americans. That common experience is sufficiently wide and deep—literature has never yet drawn even with it and can never exhaust it. In it lies the future of American literature, possibly a great future, but only as the writers of the future, by their own wit or by the grace of God, may, as the writers between wars in the main did not, accept it as their own.[35]

As he had insisted in the beginning, DeVoto had no systematized literary theory; but he believed passionately in the significance of the American past. He believed in fact, not theory; study, not ignorance; knowledge, not "guesses, phantasies, and deductions." He believed that knowledge comes only through humility. And he insisted that a really great literature will develop in America only when America is pictured as she really is. He believed in the possibility of such a literature, but he did not believe its development to be easy. As in his novels, his works on Mark Twain, and his criticism, DeVoto emphasized in his historical writing the development of America, and he based what he wrote on a vast accumulation of minute factual details. The meaning of America, he believed, was to be understood in relation to the American frontier, to the Westward Movement.

## CHAPTER 4

# Frontier Historian

**B**ERNARD DeVOTO was always a historian of the American West, even when the history was disguised in fiction or in social criticism. He began his appraisal of the impact of the frontier on American life in his first novel, *The Crooked Mile,* in the scholarly histories written by the fictional historian, John Gale. Of DeVoto's first four books, as has been noted, the first three are novels, concerned with the American frontier complex, and the fourth, *Mark Twain's America,* is social history, an impassioned defense of the West and its impact on American institutions and American writers.

In the June, 1939, *Harper's,* in the "Easy Chair," DeVoto noted Allan Nevins' suggestion that historians were pretty dull writers. DeVoto had always thought of them as "splendid as the blond Indians who, in the legends of the Southwest, were some day going to appear and free the Zuni and the Pueblo and restore the ancient glories of their race," and was disheartened that Nevins considered the blond gods as "only Diggers coated with whitewash."

Although DeVoto agreed that history was not always written as it should have been, he did not agree with Nevins that history should be written by professional journalists and that a journal of popular history should be established. He did not believe that popular history would pay unless sensationalism were practiced. Though few historians, he wrote, were lively writers, histories (and he cited Paxson's *History of the American Frontier*) were interesting. He believed that there were few good histories written by literary men, for to him the historian's love for facts would preclude such writing.

He did believe, however, that exploration and synthesis of historical facts were lacking in the writing of American history because the historian was averse to making value judgments. He believed that first-rate historians should resume the function of value judgment. If they could do this, he wrote, there would be "no move to supplement the *American Historical Review* with a periodical modeled on the *National Geographic Magazine*."[1] It is interesting that in 1943 DeVoto, a literary man, wrote a history such as he in 1939 considered impractical. Moreover, *American Heritage* seems to fit the picture of the impractical magazine.

## I   *The Frontier in History*

*Mark Twain's America* is probably the most significant of DeVoto's works. It was, as has been seen, the cause of his becoming in 1938 the curator of the Mark Twain papers, and it also contributed to his conflict with contemporary critics and to *The Literary Fallacy*. The chief contribution of *Mark Twain's America*, however, was its providing a technique for DeVoto for the writing of history. In his foreword to the book he stated that Arthur Schlesinger, Sr., had suggested that the book was the social history of Mark Twain; but DeVoto insisted that the book was not comprehensive enough to be history.[2] Nevertheless, the broad, sweeping description of the frontier from the Mississippi River to the Pacific Ocean, as it was during Twain's time, is social history of the finest kind; for the account is filled with minute detail about the daily life, the attitudes, and especially the humor of the frontiersman.

DeVoto had already contributed a thirty-five-page essay to *The Taming of the Frontier*, edited by Duncan Aikman (1925). He had reviewed numerous books about the Western frontier, including Paxson's *History of the American Frontier* in the *Evanston News-Index* and in the *Chicago Evening Post Literary Review*, and works by Mary Austin, Owen P. White, John G. Neihardt, Hartley Alexander, C. F. Lummis, Struthers Burt, and other interpreters of the West.[3] He had also recently edited the "Americana Deserta Series," which included the classic *Tall Tales of the Southwest*, by Franklin J. Meine, and *The Life and Adventures of James P. Beckwourth*, edited by T. D. Bonner (DeVoto contributed a preface and an introduction to this work).[4]

In chronological order, DeVoto's histories are *The Year of Decision: 1846* (1943), *Across the Wide Missouri* (1947), and

*The Course of Empire* (1952). He also edited and wrote an introduction to *The Journals of Lewis and Clark* (1953). Still unpublished is "Western Paradox," a volume about the twentieth-century West, which Wallace Stegner says is, except for one "Easy Chair" essay (there were actually two such essays), still in rough draft and which Mrs. DeVoto has decided not to publish.[5]

## II  The Year of Decision

The first three titles, which form the bulk of DeVoto's historical writing, are really a trilogy which explains the impact of the frontier on American civilization. *The Year of Decision,* as the title indicates, is a complete picture of what happened in all parts of America in the most interesting year of the century's most significant decade, the 1840's. Not only did DeVoto relate historical events, but he drew vigorous conclusions, also. For instance, he concluded that "at some time between August and December, 1846, the Civil War had begun."[6]

The "Calendar for the Years 1846-1847" at the beginning of the book relates only the most important events of a nineteen-month period. These events include Fremont's activities in California (where gold at Sutter's fort was soon to be discovered), The Mexican War, the Mormon trek west, the Magoffins' trip to Santa Fe, the Donner tragedy, Francis Parkman's sojourn among the Sioux, and the Mormon Battalion's trip to California. The book itself touches on the lives of almost every important person living in 1846, from Abraham Lincoln to the Brook Farmers, from Jim Bridger to Henry David Thoreau. DeVoto made an attempt to give a complete picture. In a note he expressed regret (almost anguish), that the stories of J. W. Abert, Lewis Garrard, and George F. Ruxton could not be woven into the narrative. If books did not have to end, he wrote, all three accounts would have been included.[7]

In his preface, DeVoto rationalized his method of narration. His original purpose, he said, was a literary one: "to realize the pre-Civil War, Far Western frontier as personal experience." However, when he began the book he found that his "friends and betters," the professional historians had failed him because they had done only specialized studies—all except Paxson. Nobody had tried to fit the parts together; for the stories to have literary value, their national orientation had to be made clear. Hence, DeVoto had to become a historian to provide the background.[8]

In 1943, the year of the publication of *The Year of Decision*, DeVoto wrote in the "Easy Chair" his version of why college freshmen were ignorant of the facts of American history. The main reason, he said, was that for the last twenty-five years the "fashionable intellectuals" and even literary men and historians had made a concentrated effort to "deny the validity of the American experience." Andrew Jackson was a poor speller; Rachel Jackson chewed tobacco; the Constitution safeguarded property; the pioneers denuded the land; capitalism was bound to collapse. These writers were attempting to prove that American civilization was low, its past lacking in nobility, and its great men corrupt. Since the American people had been told that the American past was one of failure and unworthiness, they were not interested in its history.

The forces at work in developing such ideas, according to DeVoto, were (1) the efforts of the professional pedagogues, who looked on history as "a socio-psychological complex," and (2) the antipathy of historians to synthesis. To DeVoto; "The facts of history are not like the facts of science; they are impure and cannot be handled with complete objectivity. Furthermore, even the most austere historian is forced to pass judgments on them, since he has to make selections, arrangements, and presentations of them."

DeVoto believed that when the professional historian refused to make value judgments the social psychologists took their place; and thus the amateur historians, who were not afraid to say something, were the only ones who were writing real history. Professional historians, he said, ruled out that which was interesting: "the narrative treatment of events, the study of personality, the resolution of problems, and above all, the free and constant expression of judgment."[9] In describing what he believed to be interesting, DeVoto described his method of writing *The Year of Decision*.

### III   The Year of Decision *as Literature*

DeVoto's *original* purpose in writing *The Year of Decision* was literary, for he did not in 1943 consider himself a historian but a literary man. He began this literary work with a quotation from a literary man; his invocation was taken from Henry David Thoreau's "Walking," an essay published in the *Atlantic Monthly* in June, 1862:

> When I go out of the house for a walk, uncertain as yet whither I will bend my steps, and submit myself to my instinct to decide for me, I find, strange and whimsical as it may seem, that I finally and inevitably settle southwest, toward some particular wood or meadow or deserted pasture or hill in that direction. My needle is slow to settle—varies a few degrees and does not always point due southwest, it is true, and it has good authority for this variation, but it always settles between west and south-southwest. The future lies in that way to me, and the earth seems more unexhausted and richer on that side. The outline which would bound my walks would be, not a circle, but a parabola, or rather like one of those cometary orbits which have been thought to be nonreturning curves, in this case opening westward, in which my house occupies the place of the sun. I turn round and round irresolute for a quarter of an hour, until I decide, for the thousandth time, that I will walk into the southwest and west. Eastward I go only by force; but westward I go free. Thither no business leads me. It is hard for me to believe that I shall find fair landscapes or sufficient wildness and freedom behind the eastern horizon. I am not excited by the prospect of a walk thither; but I believe that the forest which I see in the western horizon stretches uninterruptedly toward the setting sun, and there are no towns nor cities in it of enough consequence to disturb me. Let me live where I will, on this side is the city, on that the wilderness, and ever I am leaving the city more and withdrawing into the wilderness. I should not lay so much stress on this fact if I did not believe that something like this is the prevailing tendency of my countrymen. I must walk toward Oregon, and not toward Europe.

It is impossible to summarize *The Year of Decision* because the book is itself a summary. DeVoto did succeed in his avowed purpose; he did picture the Far Western Frontier as "personal experience." He used the technique of the novelist, and he planned and described his settings carefully. He described his characters fully; he reproduced them from original primary sources and from the records of those who were present. For example, Susan Magoffin's own journal was the basis of DeVoto's full-length portrait of her. Very little of his own imagination was used; the historian in DeVoto demanded a high degree of accuracy.

DeVoto spent a great deal of space on the journeys of Francis Parkman. He found Parkman's reactions fascinating—and always wrong. Parkman's purpose in going to the West was to study the Indians in their native state—and he did so. But he also witnessed a part of the important migration of 1846, although his book was misnamed *The Oregon Trail*. DeVoto the Westerner was not in sympathy with Parkman the Boston Brahmin:

> It was Parkman's fortune to witness and take part in one of the greatest national experiences, at the moment and site of its occurrence. It is our misfortune that he did not understand the smallest part of it. No other historian, not even Xenophon, has ever had so magnificent an opportunity: Parkman did not even know that it was there, and if his trip to the prairies produced one of the exuberant masterpieces of literature, it ought instead to have produced a key work of American history. But the other half of his inheritance forbade. It was the Puritan virtues that held him to the ideal of labor and achievement and kept him faithful to his goal in spite of suffering all but unparalleled in literary history. And likewise it was the narrowness, prejudice, and mere snobbery of the Brahmins that insulated him from the coarse, crude folk who were the movement he traveled with, turning him shuddering away from them to rejoice in the ineffabilities of Beacon Hill, and denied our culture a study of the American empire at the moment of its birth. Much may be rightly regretted, therefore. But set it down also that, though the Brahmin was indifferent to Manifest Destiny, the Puritan took with him a quiet valor which has not been outmatched among literary folk or in the history of the West.[10]

Thus DeVoto the literary man wrote history critical of the historian who produced an "exuberant masterpiece of American literature" instead of the thoughtful social history he should have written. DeVoto's frustration at Parkman's nearsightedness, however, did not permit him to deny the literary value of *The Oregon Trail*. And DeVoto's analysis of Parkman's character, including his speculation about the cause of Parkman's illness, is one of the better characterizations in the book.

## IV   *The Techniques of the Novelist*

Using the technique of the omniscient novelist, DeVoto brought together his cast of characters and fitted them all into his structure, or plot—the picturing of the parallel events of 1846, events which led to the forming of the nation: the Mexican War and the Westward Movement.

Omens are also a part of *The Year of Decision*. It had pleased DeVoto to begin *Mark Twain's America* (and end it) with the appearance of Halley's comet, which was seen in America in 1835, the year of Mark Twain's birth, and again in 1910, the year of his death. Mark Twain himself was fascinated by the fact that he "had come in on" Halley's comet and predicted that he would "go out on" it.[11]

One omen is recorded by John T. Hughes, a cavalryman in the First Missouri Mounted Volunteers, who had a bachelor of arts degree and was a schoolmaster. Early in the spring of 1846, Hughes later wrote, after a prairie thunderstorm passed over a party of traders on the Santa Fe Trail, they cried out with one voice: an image of an eagle was spread across the sun. This meant, according to Hughes's memory, that "in less than twelve months the eagle of liberty would spread his broad pinions over the plains of the west, and that the flag of our country would wave over the cities of New Mexico and Chihauhau."[12]

But DeVoto looked for a more significant omen: Biela's comet, which was observed on the earth every seven years, was seen in America in 1846. Most significantly, when scientist Matthew Maury looked at the comet through a telescope at the Naval Observatory, Biela's comet had split in two. If historian Hughes saw in the eagle spread across the sun an omen of Manifest Destiny, historian DeVoto saw in the splitting of Biela's comet Manifest Destiny on two fronts: the military front of the Mexican War and the civilian front of the Westward migration.[13]

## V   *Expansion: Manifest Destiny*

DeVoto stated that Martin Van Buren was not renominated by the Democrats in 1844 because he opposed the annexation of Texas. On the other hand, James K. Polk, who understood the American mind better than either Van Buren or his Whig opponent Henry Clay, was elected on a platform which promised the acquisition of Texas and Oregon. Moreover, Polk also believed that the American people wanted New Mexico and California. The desire for expansion had revived in America.[14]

DeVoto believed that earlier historians had missed some of the significance of expansionism when they had divided the movement into three components: the desire of the South for new lands, the need of the North and South to control the Middle West, and the "blind drive of industrialism." These forces were present, but so was another force.

> But society is never simple or neat, and our elder historians who thus analyzed it forgot what their elders had known, that expansionism contained such other and unanalyzable elements as romance, Utopianism, and the dream that men might yet be free. It also contained another category of ingredients—such as the logic of geography, which the map of January 1, 1846, made quite clear to the Americans then as it does to anyone today. You yourself, looking at a map in which Oregon was jointly occupied by a foreign power and all of the rest of the continent west of Texas and the continental divide was foreign territory, would experience a feeling made up of incompletion and insecurity. Both incompletion and insecurity were a good deal more alive to the 1840's than anything short of invasion could make them now. And finally, expansionism had acquired an emotion that was new—or at least signified by a new combination. The Americans had always devoutly believed that the superiority of their institutions, government, and mode of life would eventually spread, by inspiration and imitation, to less fortunate, less happy peoples. That devout belief now took a new phase: it was perhaps the American destiny to spread our free and admirable institutions by action as well as by example, by occupying territory as well as by practicing virtue. . . . For the sum of these feelings, a Democratic editor found, in the summer of '45, one of the most dynamic phrases ever minted—Manifest Destiny.[15]

This belief, DeVoto wrote, was the center of American faith, the force which motivated many of the soldiers and emigrants of 1846. This faith was typical of the 1840's. The Brook Farmers disapproved of it but believed it a part of a providential plan. Polk believed in it and set out to acquire the Western lands.[16]

## VI   *DeVoto's Method*

If history is merely a compilation of dates and events, then *The Year of Decision* is history. Too frequently the writers of history are bound by these facts of history; and the result is dusty, dry, and unpalatable. DeVoto said that "most historians and most scholars appear to write with something between a bath sponge and an axe." Sometimes the would-be historian, repelled by the taste of the dry-as-dust history, engages in wild flights of fancy, imagines the thoughts of his characters, and repeats conversations heard only by the conversers. But DeVoto wrote neither of these kinds of history. In *The Year of Decision,* a broadly projected and carefully executed history of one year in America, DeVoto, without distorting his material, used his skill in narration and in character development to write history that is *alive.* Few people of importance who lived in 1846 are ignored; all are fitted into the main stream of the events of that crucial year.

DeVoto's method is revealed in his description of the people of the 1840's:

> That, at least, is where one man comes out after trying to understand these people by way of what they did, what they believed, and what they felt—by way of their literature, their journalism, their religion, their causes, their institutions, their dreads, hopes, pleasures and ambitions. They were an inchoate people between two stages of the endless American process of becoming a nation, with their heads down and their eyes resolutely closed to the desperate realities which a few years would force them to confront in the deadliest of awakenings. They were a people without unity and with only a spasmodic mutual awareness, at this moment being pulled farther asunder by the centrifugal expansion of the frontier and the equal explosiveness of the developing industry—both of which would turn back again in the nation-making curve, but not for a long while yet.[17]

The major literary figures of the time, wrote DeVoto, did not express the tenor of the time; but "Stephen Foster caught it dead center. . . . The way to understand the persons who were about to fight an unpremeditated war and by building new homes in the West push the nation's boundary to the Pacific—is to steep yourself in Stephen Foster's songs."[18] "Doo-Dah Day" and "Oh Susannal"—not "Passage to India," "Eldorado," or "Roger Malvin's Burial"—are DeVoto's chapter headings.

One must read carefully *The Year of Decision* in order to understand its completeness and to appreciate its vivid characterization and narration. DeVoto's mind and his wit were constantly active; his prejudices frequently appeared. He was bemused with Francis Parkman's lack of perception. He was constantly seeking an evaluation of the contributions of the Mormons, for whom he had no love, to Manifest Destiny. He analyzed the political and military battles in depth. He presented the attitudes of the Mexicans, especially the Californios, to American occupation. He sought an explanation of the horrors experienced by the Donner Party. He defended Stephen Watts Kearney's activities in California and wrote with scorn of the politics of John C. Fremont and his father-in-law, Thomas Hart Benton. He defended (and used) Walter Prescott Webb's discussion of the importance of Samuel Colt's revolver in the winning of the West. He speculated that the source of the Civil War rebel yell was the "cry of the cattle range, a wild, unnerving sound deep in the bass which climbed to a full-throated, deafening falsctto" produced by Texans of Taylor's army who "had worked the great herds of Texas longhorns."[19]

DeVoto was not afraid of tearing down idols and of disagreeing with the critics. He spoke of "Hawthorne's exquisitely engraved melancholy" and of "the cheap gloom of Edgar Poe."[20] He praised Clarence King who, he said, survived "as a name to be mentioned in appraisals of our civilization through his friendship with a person of considerably inferior intelligence, Henry Adams. . . ." He praised Ferdinand Vandiveer Hayden, an obscure geologist who made many maps for the Geological Survey headed by John Wesley Powell, another unappreciated "prime intelligence." He admired one of Powell's assistants, Clarence Edwards Dutton; and he slyly accused Charles Dudley Warner, John Muir, and John Burroughs of plagiarizing Dutton's works: in copying whole pages exactly, they were "too absorbed to inclose them in quotation marks."[21]

After describing Congress' declaring a war which already existed, DeVoto wrote, "The muse of history does not sleep: that day an organization of superintendants of insane asylums convened in Washington."²² On the other hand, in quite another vein, DeVoto described the westering pioneer thus:

> So he had found the West and given it to the United States; now he faced the labor of subduing it and building in it a farther portion of the United States. To that labor would be addressed the rest of Bill Bowen's life and the lives of his children and their children. Christmas along the Sacramento and the Willamette, the Bay of San Francisco, the lower Columbia, was Christmas in a strange land firelit by memories of Christmas back home in the States but also heightened by the realization he had achieved. Beside these waters that fell into the Pacific there was a hope about the future that has become a deed within our past.²³

## VII   Across the Wide Missouri

The second work in DeVoto's trilogy is more than a history; it is a work of art. It is, as the preface indicates, a treatment of "the Rocky Mountain fur trade during the years of its climax and decline"—the period between 1832 and 1838. The book contains a separate chronology of the mountain fur trade; a separate article entitled "The First Illustrators of the West"; notes at the back, chapter by chapter, similar to those in *The Year of Decision;* and, most important, an extensive bibliography of works about the mountain fur trade. In addition, the book contains reproductions, some in color, of eighty-one paintings by Alfred Jacob Miller, Charles Bodmer, and George Catlin, artists who were in the West during the time covered by the book and who painted forts, mountain men, Indians, the flora and fauna of the Rockies, and the beautiful scenery.

Two facts must be taken into consideration in the analysis of this work which, as art, is the best book of the trilogy. First, DeVoto disclaimed any attempt to write a comprehensive history; he stated that Chittenden's *The American Fur Trade of the Far West* (1902) was out of date because of the uncovering of much new material, and that it was time for someone to write a modern historical synthesis. But, he insisted, *Across the Wide Missouri* was not such a history: "Instead I have tried to describe the mountain fur trade as a business and as a way of life: what its characteristic experiences were, what conditions governed them, how it helped to shape our heritage, what its relation was to the western expansion of the United States, most of all how the mountain men lived."[24]

DeVoto did admit, in his preface, that he was a historian; but he also insisted that his book was written to entertain the general reader. As a historian, he had been interested in the "growth among the American people of the feeling that they were properly a single nation between two oceans: in the devlopment of ... the continental mind." He was especially interested in relating the fur trade to westward expansion as a whole: "I shall have succeeded if the reader gets from the book a sense of time hurrying on while between the Missouri and the Pacific a thousand or so men of no moment whatever are living an exciting and singularly uncertain life, hurrying one era of our history to a close, and thereby making possible another one, one which began with the almost seismic enlargement of our boundaries and consciousness of which I have written elsewhere."[25]

The second fact that one must consider in order to evaluate DeVoto's statements about his own work is that this book, unlike *The Year of Decision,* does contain an extensive bibliography. In the first book DeVoto stated in general what his sources were, but he insisted that a complete bibliography was impossible. The implication was that this kind of history, if it were history, needed no bibliography. In *Across the Wide Missouri,* however, DeVoto provided what was unfortunately missing in the first volume. (In *The Course of Empire* [1952], DeVoto gave a bibliography, divided into "documentary" and "secondary" sources, for each chapter; but he also stated that he had made no attempt to give a full bibliography and expressed the plaintive wish that books could be written without footnotes.)

## VIII   The Mountain Fur Trade

In spite of the disclaimer in his preface, *Across the Wide Missouri* is history of the finest kind, not the "dry bones moved from one graveyard to another" (J. Frank Dobie's definition of a doctoral dissertation, with which DeVoto would agree). And DeVoto again brought to history the techniques of the novelist. The story of the mountain fur trade was constructed around the experiences of Sir William Drummond Stewart, with whom Alfred Jacob Miller traveled. Stewart was in the area for six

years, from 1833 through 1838. At the beginning of the book
DeVoto gave a "Dramatis Personae," a list of those involved in
the business during the years which the book covers. The list
reads like an honor roll (if *honor* is the right word) of the
"mountain men," the Rocky Mountain beaver trappers, who were
as nearly savage as any group on the frontier. Among those listed
are Francis Chardon, Jim Beckwourth, Jim Bridger ("Old
Gabe"), Tom Fitzpatrick, Joe Meek, Louis Vasquez ("Old Vas-
kiss"), Kit Carson, the Sublettes, Doc Newell, and Joseph Thing.
More respectable and less savage were Kenneth McKenzie of
Astor's Company, Dr. John McLoughlin of the Hudson's Bay
Company, Captain Benjamin Louis Eulalie de Bonneville of the
United States Army, Nathaniel Jarvis Wyeth (Yankee business-
man with eager beaver aspirations), Dr. Benjamin Harrison,
Captain Stewart (above), and the painter, Alfred Jacob Miller.

## IX   *Narrative Techniques*

DeVoto described the setting of his narrative well (the paintings help); the narrative has unity since most of the events are
related directly to Stewart's experiences. The point of view of
the narrative is as consistent as is possible in an effort of such a
broad scope. Although DeVoto has been criticized for presenting
a confusing story, a careful examination of the material reveals
a tight, systematic organization. The approach is as chronological
as he could make it, especially if one considers the mass of the
material presented.

And in characterization DeVoto again used his skill as a writer
of fiction. Captain Stewart is fully-drawn, as is Captain Bonneville (DeVoto is one of the few American critics to recognize
the value of Washington Irving's Western chronicles, especially
his *Captain Bonneville*). Perhaps the trapper himself, as typified
by Jim Bridger, Joe Meek, and Kit Carson, could have been
better drawn; but Irving and Ruxton had already described these
men fully. Also, modern novelists, such as Oliver La Farge and
A. B. Guthrie, Jr., have utilized Ruxton's and Irving's works in
describing the mountain man.

Extremely well drawn are DeVoto's portraits of the early mis-
sionaries to the Indians and of their wives—especially those of
their wives:

Nez Perces and trappers flung themselves to the ground and shook hands with their friends—but only for a moment. They had to gape at the most inconceivable sight ever seen there, the first white women who had come to the mountains.

Two of them. In heavy boots and swathed with yards of skirt. Riding sidesaddle. Eliza Spalding, tall, naturally thin and emaciated by illness, dark-haired, sallow under her tan, frightened and appalled by the uproar of hospitality. And Narcissa Whitman who was neither frightened nor appalled—she was delighted. A smaller woman than Eliza but by no means emaciated, the period's ideal in womanly curves, blue-eyed, tanned now but memorably blond. Men always remembered her face and her red-gold hair. Men in fact remembered Narcissa, and though she was dedicated to God's service she was charged with a magnetism whose nature no one could mistake. The Nez Perces had never seen a white woman. Joe Meek and the three equally gnarled trappers who rode with him had not seen one for years. They had their memories and their fantasies and Narcissa fulfilled them.

There are significant scenes in Western history but few so significant as this moment of uproar and wonder in a sagebrush sea. A Sioux chief is supposed to have once said that his people were not alarmed till they saw plows in the emigrant wagons and his remark has served innumerable chroniclers who may forget that the Sioux had no way of knowing what a plow was. A truer symbol would be these two women surrounded by Indians and men in buckskin, in Oregon, west of the Continental Divide.[26]

DeVoto the novelist was charmed by the contrast between the two women and also by Spalding's background—he was the illegitimate son of a woman who was herself a bastard. His description of Narcissa's wedding (full-blooded, almost spinster, dressed in black) is good. Furthermore, DeVoto recognized the dramatic possibilities of the fact that Spalding had grown up in Narcissa's home town, had worshipped at the same church, had courted Narcissa, and had been rejected by her:

Now, married in a true union of souls to the twice-born, guilt-ridden Eliza Hart, he [Spalding] was going to help establish the Oregon mission as a subordinate to Marcus Whitman, who had succeeded where he had failed. And he was privileged to travel west with the lost Narcissa on her honeymoon. Even before they reached the frontier Spalding undertook, for holiness' sake, to bring her and others to a realization of the evil in her character and to help her root it out so that God's grace might enter in.[27]

DeVoto was also unable to ignore the drama of the intricate competition of the various fur companies in the West. More than that, he saw that the missionary attempts among the Indians (for the glory of God) and the beaver trade (for the service of Mammon) were, consciously or unconsciously, aimed in one direction —Manifest Destiny. DeVoto gave as an example Jason Lee, a Methodist missionary who saw at a glance that the Flatheads were not going to become Methodists, for he could not bring their souls to Christ. They moved him to compassion—and to despair and an "overwhelming, overmastering disgust." In a letter to his nephew, written four years after Lee had decided to go on to Oregon, he said, "The truth is they are *Indians*." DeVoto says that Lee realized that in order to Christianize the Indians one first had to make white men out of them. Therefore, he went to the Willamette Valley, set up his mission, and sought to serve God by "making farmers, carpenters, herdsmen, users of soap, teetotallers, hymn-singers, monogamists, and newspaper readers of whatsoever Indians he might find there."[28]

To DeVoto, Lee, like the trappers, was a servant of Manifest Destiny:

> The time-spirit, it has been remarked, ran in Jason Lee's veins so clearly that it can be seen throbbing in his pulse. History has no accidents; Jason Lee and Hall J. Kelley, the prophet of Oregon colonization and the first American known to have proposed that the Indians of the Northwest Coast be Christianized, reached Oregon in a dead heat. Thereafter Jason Lee, in a devotion of spirit which cannot be questioned for a moment, served Christian salvation in ways indistinguishable from the promotion of real estate. The missionary to the Flatheads labored to build the City of God as a colonizer of the Willamette Valley.
>
> He was, that is, like the mountain men and Nathaniel Wyeth, an instrument of the national will. It was Jason Lee who, on July 4, 1834, at Ham's Fork, Wyoming, directed his assistants to pack up the outfit and prepare, not to travel with the Flatheads to Montana, but to go on to the Columbia with Wyeth. It was Jason Lee who gave the orders but it was Manifest Destiny that cast the vote.[29]

Lee, DeVoto bluntly stated, had the answer to the problem. Men like Marcus Whitman, who was shocked at Lee's betrayal of his trust, were wrong. Whitman tried to teach the Flatheads and the Nez Perces his brand of Christianity, complicated as it was; but Lee tried to civilize them first. Eventually Narcissa and Marcus Whitman, along with thirteen others, were massacred by the Cayuse Indians. Lee's enterprise was successful. Manifest Destiny was served.[30]

## X  *The Frontier and Government*

Thus *Across the Wide Missouri* is closely related to DeVoto's constant theme. It is noteworthy that during the years following the publication of this book DeVoto began to press his battle to preserve the remaining public lands against the encroachments of private enterprise. In *Across the Wide Missouri,* after commenting on the stupidity of those who insist that in 1837 the government should have halted Indian trade and vaccinated the Indians against smallpox, he wrote:

As for compelling or persuading any great number of Indians to submit to the insertion of a certainly diabolic medicine in a scratch on their arms, consult the records of religious missions and then of scientific foundations that have tried to deal with the neolithic mind all over the world. Including the rural white population of the southern United States in the twentieth century.

We have here a specimen of *a posteriori* thinking that corrupts history, as no one knows better than the historian of frontier societies, who has to cut his trace through an undergrowth of twentieth-century ideas projected backwards, usually with indignation. Take, since it does not involve Indians, the notion that the westward-making American pioneer culpably, and to the loss of posterity, destroyed the forests of the Middle West. It is the cornerstone of belief in every mind entitled to call itself liberal and it is taught in the very grade schools of the nation. Well, in the first place, the pioneer did no such thing. He cut down portions of the forests in order to get fields, thereby increasing the productivity of what remained. If the pioneers who made clearings for farms had been the only people who cut down trees, the forests of northern mid-America would probably be healthier today than when the frontier reached them and the problems of flood and erosion would be about what they were in 1800. (That is to say, pretty serious.) What leveled the forests was not the farmers but industry—the oil industry which wanted barrels, the railroad industry which wanted ties, and the lumber industry which wanted boards and planking.[31]

DeVoto also raised some questions: how could the conservation of soil and natural resources have been enforced, even communicated to the pioneer? How could any control have been exercised since the American ideas of natural resources, private property, the public domain, and the future were what they were? He conceded that the British monopoly system in the fur trade worked better, but he also insisted that a government-regulated monopoly in the first half of the nineteeth century was impossible. The government itself could not have conducted the trade.

For the evils in the Western fur trade, DeVoto wrote, conditions in the West were responsible. He pictured the frontier as Turner had in 1893, and then concluded that Western law had to be made up as the frontier moved. Also, the West has always been exploited by absentee Eastern owners, and the Indians, "a neolithic people in conflict with a higher culture," were "the first victims of a developing system whose later and successive victims have been white." The violence with which the Indians were handled, DeVoto wrote, was deplorable; but, in order to write accurate history, he had to relate that violence to the less murderous but nevertheless existing violence of the white society of the West. To DeVoto, "Historians of the West have not yet completed that preliminary step. This narrative calls attention to the fact that historical judgments must be peripheral or inane until the preliminaries of historical statement have been made and now feels free to return to its job."[32] DeVoto was still not writing history; he was merely suggesting in his narrative how it ought to be written.

In 1949, after the publication of *Across the Wide Missouri*, DeVoto discussed the historical method of Francis Parkman in an "Easy Chair" article. Parkman, he said, worked like a novelist, for he used the narrative approach and description of character. His history, thus, resembled fiction. This, DeVoto believed, was as it should have been, since history as literature affects men's thinking and since historians who communicate must deal with literary problems. He stated that most good historical writers were academic people and that most academic historians wrote poorly.[33]

## XI   The Course of Empire

In the third book of his historical trilogy, *The Course of Empire* (1952), DeVoto came closer to being a historian's historian than in the other two books. In his "acknowledgements" he admits to being a historian of the Westward Movement, but in his preface he calls the book the "last of three narrative studies." There is a difference, however, between the third volume and the other two: *The Year of Decision: 1846* covers less than a two-year time span; *Across the Wide Missouri*, about seven years; *The Course of Empire* (DeVoto says), a period of two hundred seventy-eight years, evidently from 1527, when Cabeza de Vaca began his long trek, to 1805, when Lewis and Clark reached the Pacific Ocean. This extended span of time made DeVoto's previous narrative approach not so "biddable." The difference in time, he wrote, made necessary "the use of different conventions, historical as well as literary, and a different method.[34] But DeVoto still insisted that literary method was a part of his approach to writing history.

This different method was a switch from the chronological narrative structure to a thematic structure; but as much as is possible with such a mass of material, the book is still a chronological history. DeVoto described his thematic method as follows:

There are minor themes but the principal ones are these: [1] the geography of North America in so far as it was important in the actions dealt with; [2] the ideas which the men involved in those actions had about this geography, their misconceptions and errors, and the growth of knowledge; [3] the exploration of the United States and Canada, so much of it as was relevant to the discovery of a route to the Pacific Ocean; [4] the contention of four empires for the area that is now the United States; [5] the relationship to all these things of various Indian tribes that affected them. Let me repeat: the meaning is not the themes in themselves but their combination.[35]

## XII   *Literary Conventions*

The different literary conventions are apparent. Individual characters could not be analyzed as minutely as in the other book, and theme rather than chronology had become the basis of structure. There is also less of the personality of the narrator in this book; in a literary sense, DeVoto had become more objective. On the other hand, there is a difference in the historical approach. In the first two books DeVoto was avowedly careful to document his statements, mainly from primary sources. In his preface to *Course of Empire* he admitted that only some of his historical facts had been established without question and that often he had given summaries of events about which there was no certainty. He had, he said, tried to be accurate; and generally, when uncertainty was present, he admitted it.[36] In spite of this honest admission of DeVoto's (or perhaps because of it), *The Course of Empire* is more "historical" than "literary." DeVoto's fifth theme by itself would make this a valuable history since few books have dealt so thoroughly with Indian troubles and Indian migrations.

According to DeVoto, the theme of all three books in the trilogy is found in Lincoln's second annual message to Congress, December 1, 1862. In this message Lincoln insisted that there was no possible national boundary in the United States which could be used for dividing the country. The line between slave and free country, Lincoln said, consisted merely of surveyors' lines or rivers easy to cross. The interior of the nation was the "great body of the Republic." Eastern, Northern, Southern, and Western outlets were necessary for trade. No boundaries were possible. DeVoto quoted in italics the following passage from Lincoln: "Our national strife springs not from our permanent part; not from the land we inhabit; not from the national homestead. There is no possible severing of this but would multiply and not mitigate evils among us. In all its adaptations and attitudes it demands union and abhors separation. In fact it would ere long force reunion, however much of blood and treasure the separation might have cost. Our strife pertains to ourselves, to the passing generations of men...."[37]

This statement of Lincoln's is, of course, a restatement of the Manifest Destiny idea of 1845, the theme of DeVoto's first two books. By the time of the Civil War it was obvious, according to Lincoln, that the United States, from the Atlantic to the Pacific Ocean, from the Canadian to the Mexican border, was destined, because of the nature of its geography, to be one nation. All five of DeVoto's themes, even the Indian migration theme, are directly related to geography; and Manifest Destiny was a geographical concept.

DeVoto also explained the apparent contradiction between Thomas Jefferson's feeling that the United States should not extend from ocean to ocean and his actions in preparing the way for such an extension to take place. DeVoto said that, if one examines Jefferson's actions in chronological sequence, from his reports on the Northwest Territory for the Congress of the Confederation to the Louisiana purchase, he must decide that, although Jefferson may sometimes have *thought* that the nation could not permanently fill its continental system, he *acted* as if, manifestly, it could have no other destiny.[38]

In 1953 DeVoto extended this thesis in an article in *Collier's.* There was significance, he thought, in the fact that Jefferson, before the purchase, secretly asked Congress to authorize the exploration of the Western area to the Pacific Ocean. (*The Course of Empire* really ends with the arrival of Lewis and Clark at the Pacific.) Moreover, Jefferson's idea that such a large area could not be governed was soon made obsolete by American inventions and development: the invention of the steamboat that could travel "in a heavy dew—or a light one, when necessary"; the development of the westward trails, such as the Santa Fe Trail, for commerce; and eventually the building of the railroads.[39]

In *The Course of Empire,* bound by the enormity of his task and by an unwillingness to ignore the facts, DeVoto nevertheless filled his account with minor mysteries and marvels. He described in detail the pursuit of many ephemera, will-o'-the-wisps such as the "Seven Cities," the "Welsh Indians," and other strange creatures just over the horizon.[40] The frontiersmen of the French, Spanish, and American frontiers are described well. He emphasized the great curiosity of the mountain men, the trappers, and the westering pioneers as to what lay behind the mountains. He posed the question of obstructions to moving west, such as the ranges of the Appalachians, and dramatized the overcoming of such obstacles. He also dramatized the Indian wars and wondered that "the Indians resisted decadence as well as they did, preserved as much as they did, and fought the whites off so obstinately and so long. For from 1500 on they were cultural prisoners." He emphasized the Indian adaptation to the horse and buffalo culture. He wrote of their use of iron in their own weapons; of the white man's adoption of the Indian's mode of transportation, the birch-bark canoe; and of the destruction of entire tribes by the white man's diseases (as when the Mandans were wiped out by smallpox).[41]

*The Course of Empire*, for which DeVoto received the 1952 National Book Award for nonfiction, is good history; and it is readable and interesting. In 1953, while he was working on *The Journals of Lewis and Clark*, DeVoto noted in the "Easy Chair" the changes that had occurred in the writing of history:

> As for Western history, for nearly twenty years an unorganized movement has been extending its content and radically changing its approaches. When another Turner or Paxson sets out to construct a generalization about the place of the westering frontier in American history, he will have at his disposal many fundamental things that his predecessors had to do without: whole categories of experience, new and different and more realistic theories and ideas and points of view. At the hands of such men as Walter Webb, Henry Nash Smith, Wallace Stegner, Joseph Kinsey Howard, Dale Morgan, George Stewart, and a good many others, Western history has been so changed and enlarged that the next Turner will produce a revolution in historiography.[42]

DeVoto did not include himself in the list, but there is no real doubt that he contributed much to the production of interesting history by helping to enliven historical writing.

### XIII   The Journals of Lewis and Clark

DeVoto's next and last important historical production was the editing of *The Journals of Lewis and Clark*, published in 1953. The book, which is a readable account, is about a third of the original edition of the journals edited by Reuben Gold Thwaites and published in 1904-5. Much of the material included by Thwaites was "essential to the purposes of the expedition but unrelated to the running narrative and a considerable drag on it." DeVoto, who omitted the "unrelated" material, made the finished narrative available to the reading public, whereas the Thwaites edition, rare and costly, was not.[43]

The essay which introduces the volume is an excellent summary of the reasons behind the expedition, although much of the material can be found in DeVoto's other works. The main addition to knowledge is DeVoto's discussion of the route of the expedition itself, in which he showed that the Lewis and Clark expedition, while settling once and for all the question of whether or not there was an easy route to the Pacific, provided a route for westward migration to Oregon. More important, the railroads which were to come later in great part followed the Lewis and Clark route to the Northwest. The expedition also served to help secure Oregon for the United States. DeVoto related the results of the expedition to his basic themes:

> But it gave not only Oregon but the entire West to the American people as something with which the mind could deal. The westering people had crossed the Mississippi with the Louisiana Purchase and by that act had acquired the manifest destiny of going on to the Pacific. But the entire wilderness expanse, more than twice the size of the United States at the beginning of Jefferson's administration, was a blank, not only on the map but in human thought. It was an area of rumor, guess, and fantasy. Now it had been crossed by a large party who came back and told in assimilable and trustworthy detail what a large part of it was. Henceforth the mind could focus on reality. Here were not only the Indians but the land itself and its conditions: river systems, valleys, mountain ranges, climates, flora, fauna, and a rich and varied membrane of detail relating them to one another and to familiar experience. It was the first report on the West, on the United States over the hill and beyond the sunset, on the province of the American future. There has never been another so excellent or so influential. So it was rather as a treasury of knowledge than as a great adventure story that the *History* [by Nicholas Biddle] became a national and international favorite, reprinted, translated, pirated, and counterfeited. It satisfied desire and it created desire: the desire of the westering nation.
>
> That, the increase of our cultural heritage, the beginning of knowledge of the American West, must be accounted the most important result of the Lewis and Clark expedition.[44]

This evaluation of the Lewis and Clark expedition is a good example of DeVoto's approach. The synthesis was made, the facts were cited, and the value of the expedition was assessed. But the phraseology, such as "a rich and varied membrane of detail" and "over the hill and beyond the sunset," is not that of the pedestrian historian but of the historian who is (consciously or unconsciously) literary.

## XIV  *Belletristic Historian*

As a historian DeVoto never managed (if he wanted to) to escape his literary background. To say that he was a literary historian would be in error; this term has been widely used to describe another type of writer, and DeVoto would not want to be so designated. Instead he was a historian constantly influenced by the literary way of thinking. While he was careful to make his history factual, he was always affected by an irrepressible imagination. Perhaps, although he would sneer at the classification and doubt its necessity, he was a belletristic historian or a belletrist surrounded by the world of historical fact.

## CHAPTER 5

# Social Historian: The Nature
# of American Civilization

## I "Farewell to Pedagogy"

WHEN DeVoto left Northwestern University in 1927 and
moved to Cambridge, Massachusetts, his "Farewell to Pedagogy" in the January, 1928, *Harper's* indicated his state of mind.
His purpose then was to make his living by writing. Except for
part-time teaching at Harvard from 1929 through 1936, he did
make a living with his pen. By 1927 he was contributing articles
to *Harper's, American Mercury,* and *Saturday Review of Literature* and short stories to the *Saturday Evening Post* and other
magazines. He wrote to sell and made no apologies for the fact;
indeed, he was quick to defend the practice.

## II The "Easy Chair"

Thus in order to get a consistent picture of DeVoto's thinking,
one must read his magazine publications. Although *Minority
Report, Forays and Rebuttals, The World of Fiction, The Hour,*
and *The Easy Chair,* as well as some of the Twain books, reprint
and sometimes expand some of them, a reading of all the magazine articles is essential. And DeVoto's greatest contribution to
quality magazine journalism was his "Easy Chair" articles and
other publications in *Harper's.*

DeVoto wrote the "Easy Chair" (four pages, double column)
for *Harper's* from November, 1935, through January, 1956—a
total of 243 issues; this was two more articles than William Dean
Howells wrote in the first two decades of the century. During
this time DeVoto wrote other significant articles for *Harper's*

and other magazines and published fifteen books, including four novels under the pseudonym John August, and a collection of articles (mainly from *Woman's Day*) under the pseudonym Cady Hewes (1956), and the three monumental histories. He was editor of the *Saturday Review of Literature* from September 26, 1936, to March 1, 1938, and after that a regular contributor. He wrote introductions to numerous books, and published book reviews in several journals and short stories under various pseudonyms as well as under his own name.

In the midst of this great amount of writing, however, the "Easy Chair" columns give a better view of DeVoto's thinking than any other source. In them are found a mature man's observations on the American scene from the end of the Great Depression through a war and a half. A summary of the subject matter of the "Easy Chair" is one, therefore, of what was going on in America from 1935 through 1955. He wrote about the state of American education (about which he was not optimistic), the foolishness of prophecy (although he made some foolish prophecies), the coming and the progress of World War II (which he prophesied accurately), the foolishness of literary censorship (a favorite topic), the New Deal, the lessons offered by the Civil War, the work of the creative writer, the failure of creative writers, the values and defects of the American automobile, the poor state of American manufactures (his chief enemy was the stainless steel kitchen knife), tourism in America, governmental wartime propaganda, the Communist scare, the work of the Dies Committee and of the Federal Bureau of Investigation, and almost any topic one could name.

In the "Easy Chair" articles there emerges a consistently sober, sane, and fair attitude toward American civilization. He was a critic, but a loving one who had great confidence in the American people and in the American system of government. He was avowedly, unashamedly patriotic, and there are two constant themes in the "Easy Chair" essays: (1) the greatness of American civilization and the weakness of its detractors and (2) the damnation of those who would destroy the public lands of the American West. Both themes are closely related to ideas that had been presented and were being presented in DeVoto's novels, Twain books, critical works, and histories.

In November, 1945, midway in his career as a writer of the "Easy Chair," DeVoto did an evaluation of his first ten years. About the previous editors he wrote, "They have talked about the fundamental continuity of American life"; and he indicated that he would continue this policy. He insisted that he had sought to avoid controversy: "I am a literary person, which is to say a conciliatory, timorous soul, given to extreme understatement in order to avoid rows, habitually moderating my opinions to the verge of anemia or beyond lest someone disagree." On the other hand, he had never been permitted to avoid controversy: "When my book on the culture of hydrangeas comes out next month, watch every reviewer find belligerence in it, unless some lonely iconoclast decides that it is about the frontier." But he still maintained that his method was sound: "I appeal to experience and I look up the facts."[1]

In the same esay he discussed the changes which America had undergone and was undergoing. He made a series of statements which might be considered a creed—an answer to the detractors of America, those who, he believed, had misunderstood the nature of the American experience:

> Let me add this, however. The rate of change in American society has always been dizzy. It is now going to have an unparalleled acceleration. But I believe that what I have been saying about it for ten years will hold from here on. That the unstable equilibrium is not flowing toward overturn or chaos but toward successive states of equilibrium. That the form is organic and functional and will contain the parts in dynamic balance. That the pattern of change is effectively determined from within, not from without, by our traditions and institutions, which are alive, and by our will, which is free. That our democracy is so much stronger than any threat which can be brought against it from outside that there is no reason to be afraid. That the truly dangerous threats to it are our own contradictions, corruptions, and moral failures. That though these make our adventure desperate and forlorn in the light of eternity, in the light of history and finite time it is absurd to despair. That our confidence is justified. That we have the best chance and that it will be enough.[2]

### III  *American Civilization*

In his evaluation of twentieth-century America, DeVoto consistently went back to the frontier as a starting point in the development of his ideas. America, he thought, must be understood in the context of its frontier origins. American democracy was a development from within and thus would survive. In a Christmas essay in 1936 DeVoto stated that the frontier and the activities of the frontier are symbolic of "the American way of life":

> Light shining on snow through winter dark is as universal as the star going before the Wise Men on their way, but also to all who have lived in America it has a special reference, being as well the light from a cabin in the clearing with the forest beyond them stretching toward the unknown West.
>
> ...And the cabin in the clearing, the clipper fleet, the departed heroes, and the corn standing in the shocks are systolic in us, part of the rhythm of our breath and of our desire—and part too of our fate. They stand for our own way of life, they are our living tradition; and we understand them, and no one else understands them. That is the way our corn is shocked.
>
> ...The cerebral people—characterized primarily by fear and by contempt of the unconsidered multitudes and by a lust for absolutes and for absolute power—tell us that America must choose between two ways of life, both European, both essentially the same, both intolerable. Let there be read to them the prayer appointed to be read in churches on Christmas Day: they are fools and liars and the truth is not in them. That is not our choice but an alien one, and our choice is foreordained for us by our own tradition; our native way of life formed by our own systole and diastole. Our corn is maize, and Europe had no maize.[3]

## IV   *The Pioneer Ideal*

DeVoto related the growth of American civilization to the pioneer ideal. The American dream, he believed, was based on the desire for security, as was the pioneering spirit. The modern American spirit, he thought, is based on the same ideal and aspirations. He deeply resented the picturing of the modern American as soft and spineless. In an essay written on the eve of World War II, he defended the American pioneer ideal:

> If the desire to make life easy for oneself and one's children is a feminine ideal, then what we call the American dream has been feminine from the beginning, and the pioneers who cleared the forests and yoked up for Oregon were puling softies. They desired a better life for themselves and their families—comfort

and security. . . . Pioneering . . . was an effort to rise in the world: to be secure in your old age, to get your children better schooling than you had had, to put a bathroom in the cabin, to put in two bathrooms, even, in that now shameful cliché, to have two cars in your garage.[4]

## V  *The Literary Man and the Frontier*

DeVoto believed that the ones responsible for the degrading of the American dream and for the picturing of the pioneer (and the modern American) as weak and spineless were the modern writers of the Lost Generation and the critics with whom he battled most of his life. As has been noted, he believed that few of the writers who had written about the frontier had really looked into the lives of "the ordinary men and women who gave value to the wilderness."[5] Besides, he wrote, few first-rate writers had remained in the West; he listed only Edwin Corle, Thomas Hornsby Ferril, Vardis Fisher, and Joseph Kinsey Howard. These men, he wrote, were strong enough to resist the forces of their time:

> . . . but that such achievement as their requires unusual strength is obvious from what has happened to the generality of Western writing. It has got mired in the spongy, self-conscious regionalism that has devitalized American writing wherever it has broken out, though for the South's forty acres and a poet the spacious West has substituted six hundred and forty acres and a mystic. Or else it has fled into coterie literature, with the result that the little magazine is making its last stand in the sagebrush and the writer who stayed there is trying to be Eugene Jolas. He has his own *Vogue* and *Spur* and is trying to erect a Left Bank on Nine Mile. This escapism is pathetic rather than vulgar because it is forced on him, but if escapism is a means of survival it nevertheless ranges him with the millionaire. He has found no roots in the common culture and so regards it as colonial.[6]

The literary men of America, DeVoto believed, had pictured America and its people as "inferior, venal, corrupt, pathological, stupid, and ridiculous" and American traditions as "trivial, inferior, and base." In 1940 he felt that the time had come to expose the lies and to insist "that the American traditions have not lost their power nor the American people their virility."[7] But DeVoto had actually been fighting this battle in the "Easy Chair" for several years. In 1938 he poked fun at certain literary people who had recently become aware of "folk" handicrafts, collecting them while disparaging the craftsmen at the same time:

> This was the master-idea of a whole generation of critics: this poverty of the American imagination, this atrophy of the American sense of beauty, this hatred of skill. A whole generation lived well—and bought Connecticut farmhouses and filled them with hand-hewn beams, Sandwich and Stiegel glass, walnut furniture, and Currier and Ives prints—by telling us in books and from the lecture platform that our grandparents were a coarse lot, though there was hope for us since we appeared willing to bear instruction. The pre-Repeal Critic who informed you that what principally distinguished American life and history was the absence of all craftsmanship, skill, and folk art, which is to say the absence of the only compost in which civilization might sprout, was pretty funny. But he is funnier now, discovering dynamic symmetry in Aunt Martha's milk skimmer, abstract design in her patchwork quilt. He is funniest of all when he accepts both notions at the same time, the beauty-hating peasant and the lowly artist through whose fingers beauty came to be.[8]

DeVoto wrote that the American "folk soul" has been interpreted by writers who claim to love the people and at the same time degrade them to "the folk." It has always taken skill, DeVoto believed, to live in America; for, the more primitive the life, the more skill required. Pioneers made artifacts of materials around them and made them beautiful whenever possible. There have never been "American folk," DeVoto believed; there were merely people "short on money and long on skill" who did not worship what they made. Those who interpret the American people should live among them.[9]

## VI   *The American Writer and American Institutions*

In 1941, DeVoto again discussed the attitude of major American writers towards American institutions. Those who had once been contemptuous had, with the approach of the war, recanted and become patriotic. What they had denounced twenty years before they now considered indispensable. The main current of American literature of the 1920's pictured Americans as an inferior race; only the misfits had made the Atlantic passage. Mencken, Brooks, Harold Stearns, Lewis Mumford, and Ludwig

Lewisohn set forth these ideas; and even Edmund Wilson accepted their attack on American culture. To DeVoto,

> This is what our official literature, the literature which writers themselves accepted, praised, and worked within. It spent ten years showing that the Americans were stripped Europeans, brutalized by their wilderness continent, malformed by the repulsive forces of the Puritan and the Pioneer, materialistic and envious and intolerant and corrupt, standardized and uniform in thought and feeling and ideal, enforcing uniformity on everyone, hating distinction and individuality, fearing freedom, denying freedom to those who were valiant enough to desire it, contemptuous of beauty, ignorant of culture and high thinking and the good life—at once the victims and the despots of the mass mind. You will remember that the literary ranged through history, folklore, and what they called the racial unconscious to prove that the Americans had always been the same, that our past was tawdry, our heroes unworthy, and our goals base. The examination was complete and the verdict absolute: the Americans were a cruel and offensive mediocrity, a herd whose will was expressed as the tyranny of the mass mind. Let us remember that what literature was talking about then was what it is talking about now as American democracy.[10]

DeVoto believed that there were some writers, such as Frost, Sandburg, Ellen Glasgow, and Willa Cather, who dealt with the American human experience honestly; but he damned Lewis, Eliot, and the Wastelanders who, he said, had condemned American democracy.

In 1942 DeVoto lambasted Dorothy Thompson for her lack of understanding of America, spending an entire "Easy Chair" essay on her shortcomings as a critic of America. He stated that Miss Thompson insisted that America's difficulties were based on "ruthless competition for power, prestige, and success" and that America was undergoing in World War II what she deserved. Miss Thompson believed that American civilization was based on a series of indefensible wars and its economy on obsolescence and fear-causing advertising. She believed that America, made weak by her luxuries, was being defeated by the Japanese and the Germans and saved by the Russians.

DeVoto, stating that it is always difficult to comment on a charge fired from a shotgun, made fun of Miss Thompson for reversing her position from glorification to condemnation of the

American system. The reason, he said, was the "intensifying Puritanism that always accompanies war." This Puritanism during World War I gave the United States prohibition, for instance. He called Miss Thompson a revivalist, a camp meeting preacher, and reminded her that America's pleasure-seekers were working hard and fighting hard. And he answered Miss Thompson in terms one might expect:

> It is too late to ask America to change its heart. We cannot, either to win the war or to satisfy Miss Thompson, go back to the beginning and start again in an expiatory conviction that our civilization is false and tawdry, that the entire history of the United States up to now has been evil. For if material abundance and the desire for it are evil, at least they have been part of the American idea from the beginning.
>
> Part of the idea was that the undernourished should find abundant food here, up to the two green vegetables and the two desserts that Miss Thompson scorns. Part of the idea was that the ill-clothed and ill-housed should have a reasonable expectation of serviceable stockings, if not silk ones, and comfortable homes, if not a house in the east Fifties. Part of the idea was that their children should have good teeth, enough vitamins to prevent rickets, and schools reasonably warm, well-lighted, and comfortably equipped. It is not and it never has been an evil idea or even an ignoble one. Until it is fully realized, idealism must remain a function exclusively of incomes large enough to afford it. It is only possible to be spiritual about green vegetables, good teeth, or even silk stockings when you have got them. And meanwhile it is extremely odd to preach the idea of material abundance to the conquered and oppressed as one of the great dawns we are preparing for them while, in the same breath and for a secure income, you denounce it to us as contemptible.[11]

## VII  *The Lost Generation*

In 1943 DeVoto asserted that post-World War I writers had not pictured army life as it was, and expressed the hope that World War II novels would. He described the recanting of the Lost Generation writers:

> But in the 1920's writers withdrew from the national life as a consciously superior caste, and that withdrawal was at once ignorant, arrogant, and dilettante. By the most diverse and dis-

cordant ways literary people arrived at a common conclusion that the American people were inferior, their institutions decadent or offensive, their ideals low, their ways of life disgusting, and their experience worth neither belief nor the attention of the anointed. Literature washed its hands of us, withdrawing into contempt, into obscurities penetrable only by the initiated, or into adoration of the coming world revolution. And this withdrawal of a superior class from things which alone give vitality to literature exacted a certain penalty. If writers in our time have been a superior class, literature has tended to be a mere frivolity, a mere aesthetics, a mere neurosis, or a mere clique. For some years, literature has been confessing its failures: the mourner's bench has been crowded with writers telling us that they now know they were wrong. The spectacle is both pathetic and humiliating. But it may suggest a moral to the ten million [veterans of World War II].[12]

DeVoto, who believed that many World War I veterans had identified themselves with the Lost Generation of the 1920's, hoped to prevent a second Lost Generation. He wrote, in a memorable description of those he held in contempt, "The Lost Generation mistake was to generalize individual failure into a law of God and to suppose that a private pain in the bowels revealed the nature of reality."[13] In another anatomical description, in answer to an adverse review of *The Literary Fallacy*, DeVoto insisted that the Lost Generation literature did not define the hopes and beliefs of American writers, nor did they speak for the pre-World War II period. DeVoto wrote, "The heart of literature is not broken; it's just that some writers have heartburn."[14]

The reason underlying the Lost Generation's contempt for the American dream and the American system, DeVoto believed, was a basic misunderstanding of the essential nature of democracy as it existed in America, a democracy fostered by and nourished on the American frontier. DeVoto described Lincoln, the frontiersman, as "the highest expression of American democracy that survived the test." In the most terrible time in American history, the Civil War, America "formed within itself the instrument [Lincoln] that was needed to save it."[15]

The Lost Generation writers, however, did not have this clear vision of the nature of the American people and of democracy. DeVoto used as an example H. L. Mencken's comments, made in 1925, as to what would happen should the United States go to war with Japan. Mencken had predicted mass panic west of Salt Lake City, slaughter of the Japanese-Americans, and hysteria in general. Ignoring the fact that Mencken was not altogether wrong, DeVoto wrote in 1943: "Mr. Mencken was engaged in literary extrapolation. He was required to forecast such behavior by his thesis about the American people: democracy as mob rule, the mob as base and cowardly, the Americans as inferior people, descendants of the rejects who alone had found the trans-atlantic migration attractive, and the nation which the inferiors built as incapable of discipline, courage and honor."

DeVoto insisted that the literary treatment of the America of the 1920's was as inaccurate as Mencken's extrapolation. There were many decent people in America in the 1920's, people who had decent ideals and aspirations. These people were not interesting to the writers, whose minds were clouded by lack of understanding: "Abstractly the literary intelligence loved the people. But concretely, it despised, feared, and hated the mob. Hence literature's fantastic interim—twenty-odd years of repudiating democracy on the ground that democracy was mob rule, government by the anarchy of the mass mind, the political systematization of envy and cowardice and greed and corruption, a decadent and doomed way of life, a rotting mess of outworn superstitions and degenerate myths."[16]

In 1937, in an essay opposing the participation of American "idealists" in the Spanish Civil War, DeVoto gave a bitter definition of the idealism that the writers he had been opposing claimed to have. These idealists—members of the Lost Generation who were in the process of finding themselves—included Hemingway and other American writers:

> Experience has derived a rule-of-thumb which seems to work: if someone tells you he is an idealist, he probably is. History provides another one: idealism is a process by which your private wish comes to be identified with eternal truth, eternal justice, or the right that must prevail. Or, more simply: idealism is the will to subjugate man in the name of humanity, and idealists are those who love the people but fear or despise the mob and so desire to subjugate it for the sake of greater things to come.

DeVoto concluded that "idealism commonly ends as the thing it sets out to destroy."[17] Two years before he had insisted that the ideal society was as impossible as the perfect automobile, because society, like the automobile, operates at a minimum level of efficiency. The politician in an inefficient society keeps things working. This, DeVoto believed, might be just as well. Men throughout the ages have been designing the perfect society, but the people have gone their own way, pragmatically working out their destinies with no reference to the ideal plans. This hit-and-miss approach, constantly changing but not necessarily improving, is typical of democracy.[18]

## VIII  *American Democracy*

DeVoto believed, therefore, that there was something unique in the democracy that was developed as America moved West. In an essay written in 1936 and published early in 1937—an attack on courses in professional education—DeVoto incidentally expressed his view on changing attitudes toward American democracy and, also incidentally, gave his definition of democracy:

> The events of the last year have shifted democracy in the United States from the defensive to the offensive. As recently as a year ago those who believed in the democratic way of doing things were under a cross-fire from both right and left, and the drunkards of absolutism seemed more self-confident than they were. . . . The reelection of Mr. Roosevelt, for instance, meant many things, but among them it meant a victory for the point of view that sees the problems of society as multiple and inter-related rather than homologous and independent. Simple solutions, absolute solutions, and uniform solutions have been at least temporarily discountenanced, and democracy is seen to be a pluralistic process of moving toward a resolution of forces, rather than a generalized and single process of moving to a goal.[19]

One of DeVoto's strongest defenses of American democracy was his essay written early in 1941 in which he made suggestions as to what kind of history should be taught ten-year-olds:

> Some of them [historians] have been telling us that the Founding Fathers distrusted democracy, tried to protect the United States from it, and cut our form of government to fit—a form of government, we will be so good as to understand, which was intended to be not a democracy but a republic. The Constitution was meant to be an osage-orange hedge to keep democracy from

spreading among us, and so long as we had the republic thus founded and protected we remained in good health. Unhappily, however, the American system has been repeatedly infected with democracy since 1788 (footnote for columnists: the year when the Constitution was ratified), and precisely those infections are what ail us now. Although plainly we are perishing because of them, we seem to be crying for still more transfusions of democracy.

DeVoto did not believe that the Founding Fathers were possessed of prophetic gifts, but that they had worked hard with what they had and with what they knew. They were, of course, limited by their ideas (the Age of Reason was not perfect) and experience:

That experience included a lifelong familiarity with a greater measure of political democracy than the world outside this continent had ever seen. When they wrote the constitution they went to the limit of that experience and a little beyond it: they wrote it to embody a still greater measure of democracy. And, yes, it is true that most of them desired no further democratization of the system they established, and within the limits of their foresight took measures which they thought would prevent it ... they created a political system flexible enough to maintain its forms and functions while it was adjusted to the experience of later generations.

For the history of the United States is, in large part, a history of the democratization of the republic established by the Fathers, which has made it not only the most secure government on earth, as it is now the oldest, but also the freest and most powerful.

DeVoto's conclusion was, therefore, that democracy succeeds. The only time when democracy could not succeed was during the "War Between the States," but he believed that America has benefited from the defeat of the Confederacy. The reason he gave involves his concept of the frontier and the idea of Manifest Destiny, the dominant motivating force in the development of America:

So our history for ten-year-olds and public thinkers will have to use clear, simple, emphatic words. The South was defeated, the North won the war, and the United States therefore became what it remains today, the bulwark of democracy and the basis of hope for the future. . . . Nevertheless, the war had to be fought for many sufficient reasons—in order, to name only one of them, that the continental nation should not be balkanized—and the victory of the North was good for the modern world. . . .

This victory was good for America, DeVoto believed, because the Civil War provided the answer to two problems left unsolved by the Founding Fathers: slavery and the class-structured agrarian economy. Because the defeat of the South destroyed these two institutions, it was a victory for democracy. The Civil War was, therefore, "the one all-out effort of an American reaction, the one last-ditch opposition to the progress of political and social democracy in the United States." The Civil War also proved that American democracy was capable of surviving any kind of attack and that the destiny of America was to survive as a democratic nation capable of making whatever changes and adjustments were necessary for progress:

> . . . The record shows that the United States has repeatedly adapted its democracy to a changing world, that its democracy is dynamic, that it keeps going. That it has been willing to take risks and has been justified in taking them. That it has opposed the forces which seemed baneful to it—successfully. That it has learned that some questions can be settled forever by war and that it is best to leave them settled in your interest. That it has been willing to go to war for self-preservation of its beliefs. That its experience proves the efficiency of democracy in war. That it has won its wars. That, on the basis of the record, it will win this one.[20]

### IX  Manifest Destiny

DeVoto seemed to believe that the concept of Manifest Destiny still survives in America, for he wrote in 1941: "A century ago Manifest Destiny was the belief of the American people that their way of life was desirable for other people and would be the more secure if other people adopted it, and we seem to have decided that they were right. It has proved to be the destiny of this generation to give Manifest Destiny a seed."[21]

As has been seen, DeVoto had a profound confidence in the American system and people. Early in the "Easy Chair" series, in the third essay, he compared the America of the 1840's with that of the 1930's: both decades were confused, socially and economically. Depression, bank failures, and business bankruptcies were rife during both periods. The decade of the 1840's was filled with solutions to the economic and social problems; the decade of the 1930's had the New Deal. An aura of doom pervaded both decades. When the essay was written, someone had just predicted a proletarian revolution in America by 1937. But society had survived the decade of the 1840's, and DeVoto believed it would survive the 1930's. America, always in a state of flux, had generally overcome all obstacles. In spite of social and economic recessions and progressions, a unique American people had always emerged. Indeed, America thrived on problems. DeVoto concluded his essay with the following pronouncement:

> The American race is a continuity. What they do, they do in their own way, with their own idiom and accent, shaping it to the habit of their hands with a skill conditioned here and nowhere else. They have not repeated the struggle for existence nor much improved upon the human race which Almighty God bungled so disastrously. . . . No one needs on New Year's Day any greater assurance than the assurance that their struggle for existence has taken its shape here from the American race and has retained that shape from generation to generation while the nation fell headlong from one seeming stability to another, as social change rocketed and swirled and skidded it beyond anyone's power to comprehend and especially to predict. It has remained a way of life certainly not beautiful or just, as beauty and justice go in the New Jerusalem, but accommodated absolutely to the Americans, stamped with their shape, issuing out of their conditions.[22]

## X  *"The American Way"*

In 1938 *Harper's* conducted a contest in an attempt to define "the American Way" and published the four prize-winning essays. The four winners emphasized four mutually exclusive theses (communism, political experiment, stability and flexibility, and multiplicity). DeVoto believed that the fourth theory was the most significant:

> It is a point of complete realism and of the greatest possible importance. If Mr. Coyle [the author of the essay] will now develop it fully through a series of essays (it would be pleasant if his colleagues in the New Deal could be required to read them) he will be performing a public service of enormous value. For what is most hallucinatory—and most discouraging and dangerous—in the debates of the day is the all but unchallenged su-

premacy of monisms. Marxism is but one of a dozen ardently supported fallacies based on the imbecile delusion that our system is single, can be operated as single, and must be upheld and displaced by singularities. . . . The reality that Mr. Coyle so well uncovers is the existence of our system as a resultant, a multiplicity of systems, more or less out of harmony, more or less at odds, but held in dynamic equilibrium.

DeVoto related the passing of the frontier to his idea of "dynamic equilibrium"; at the same time he gave an early example of the use of the phrase "the new frontier," although some might disagree with his definition: "Similarly, when told that the passing of the frontier has been a decisive change in the constituents of the equilibrium, a bystander's first comment is that a greater change shows in our current desire to solve questions politically rather than institutionally. The new frontier is Washington, the new ethics are political, the new constituents are gangs—none of them wholly new but all of them stepped up by enormous induction."[23]

During his twenty years of writing for the "Easy Chair," DeVoto was a staunch defender of democracy, which, in summary, he believed was developed on the frontier and nurtured in American freedom. He believed that "the American Way," which he understood to be a development of Manifest Destiny, was admirable because it was a flexible system. He did not regard government or social structures in absolute terms; he had supreme confidence in the ability of the American people, nurtured in a comparatively free society, to solve their problems. In 1950, three-fourths of the way through his career as editor of the "Easy Chair," DeVoto wrote an impassioned defense of American democracy; and he finished it with a typical statement:

Sure the people are stupid: the human race is stupid. Sure Congress is an inefficient instrument of government. But the people are not stupid enough to abandon representative government for any other kind, including government by the guy who knows. They have just had to fight their worst war to get three such governments out of the way, and may have to fight another one to dispose of the fourth. And bad as our system is, it is more effective than those governments. Their system has been tried repeatedly since Plato (a little liberal who understood that people are stupid) first proposed it and in the end it never works.

They are efficient at starting wars but not much else. I'd rather have efficiency at finishing them, as we have always shown we have, and at keeping the train on the tracks, as we have done. It may be a crude criterion but we are the oldest form of government now operative: we have outlasted every other political system in the world.[24]

## CHAPTER 6

# Reformer: The Plundered Province

DESPITE his statements to the contrary, Bernard DeVoto obviously loved controversy. In *Harper's* (August, 1934), he wrote a long essay entitled "The West: A Plundered Province," in which he accused Eastern forces of destroying the West: he included in his accusations the mine owners, the railroads, the banks, and the land speculators. The West was destroyed, he said, to enrich Eastern speculators and absentee owners. Obviously the product of the research done for *The Crooked Mile* and *The House of Sun-Goes-Down,* the essay set the tone for DeVoto's later writing and perhaps provided a catchy phrase to describe what he felt was the condition of the West. Thus early in his career he manifested an interest in the problem of conservation and defense of the Western lands from exploitation by outside (and local) financial interests.[1]

During the period from 1935, when he began writing the "Easy Chair" essays, to late in 1945, he kept an eye on what was going on in the Western states and reported what he considered to be attempts to destroy the government lands of the West, a part of the American inheritance. Then early in 1944, in a review of several books about the West, he began to tell the American people the "facts of life" about the Intermountain West. As an aside in *The Literary Fallacy,* published that year, he noted that only the federal government could develop some of the Western areas.

## I  *"The Anxious West"*

In the summer of 1946 DeVoto made a trip through the West, along the route of the Lewis and Clark expedition. Four "Easy

Chair" essays of that year are about the Western trip, but he made few specific comments on Western conditions. These comments were evidently being reserved for two major articles, "The Anxious West" for the December, 1946, *Harper's* and "The West Against Itself" for the January, 1947, issue. The first essay, relatively mild, sets forth a background of facts and makes some mildly controversial statements. But in the January issue DeVoto's article was the lead one (the December article had been printed at the back of the magazine), and it was eventually reprinted in *The Easy Chair* (1955), which contains several of the conservationist articles. The article was packed with facts; DeVoto named names and described legislative programs which he believed would destroy the Western economy.

In the same issue, January, 1947, DeVoto used the "Easy Chair" as a platform from which to make an impassioned plea for soil and forest conservation. For the rest of his life in the pages of *Harper's* he fought the battle against exploitation and despoiling of the West's natural resources. In his first article of the twenty-first year of his tenure in the "Easy Chair" (only two more articles appeared), DeVoto, in his analysis of his twenty years as "Easy Chairman," said that his articles in *Harper's* had been the only adequate coverage of the struggle over the public lands from January, 1947, on.[2]

A year earlier DeVoto expressed the belief that the battle had been just about won, but during the year he warned that Americans must ever be on the watch.[3] Arthur M. Schlesinger, Jr., gives DeVoto sole credit for bringing the big public lands steal to a sudden halt by arousing public opinion against the various attempts to scuttle the federal government's conservation program.[4]

DeVoto's stand on the public lands question incurred the hatred of many Westerners, despite the fact that he himself was a Westerner. In 1948, when his hostess at a party asked him, "How have you gotten away so long with being a professional Westerner?," DeVoto was amused, because at that very time the Western press was united in berating him. A Denver columnist had recently declared that DeVoto hated the West; a Nevada paper had entitled a criticism of his *Harper's* article "Cow Dung," and he had been called a "paid propagandist" and a foreigner.[5]

One reason DeVoto was disliked by the newspapers and the political groups of the West was that in the heat of the controversy, in the period after 1947, he drew lines, not between East and West, but between large corporations and individuals, between the cattleman and the "pioneer." His attack upon the ranching industry, as well as the range cattle industry, was bitter. It was to be expected that the answers would also be bitter.

## II  *Industry as Destroyer*

In *Across the Wide Missouri,* published in 1947, DeVoto, as has been noted, stated the forests of Northern mid-America had not been destroyed by the pioneer farmer but by industry, which demanded barrels for oil, cross-ties for railroad tracks, and lumber for sale. In 1944, in a review of a book about life in the Middle West, DeVoto said about the author:

> Thus in a sentence or two he demolishes a favorite myth of deplorers, that the ignorant pioneers destroyed the forests. They did not destroy the forests, they merely burned some trees to make fields and cut down other trees for use. The clearing of farms and the establishment of Mid-western agriculture hardly scratched the great forests. Not even the first generation of industry and the building of railroads seriously impaired them. They disappeared only when the rise of the petroleum industry converted oak trees to barrel staves by the billion.[6]

The Western institution which contributed most to the destruction of natural resources, according to DeVoto, was the cattle industry. In the 1944 essay just cited, he stated that the two destructive forces in Montana were the cattle kingdom and the Amalgamated Copper Company, which owned the state. In "The Anxious West," the first of the two major *Harper's* essays, DeVoto wrote: "Increasingly the West sees itself as congeries of big cow outfits before the freeze of 1886." He believed that the West's picture of itself had been strongly influenced by Hollywood: "The most significant aspect of this revelation is that the West has chosen to base its myth on the business that was of all Western businesses most unregardful of public rights and decencies, most exploitative, and most destructive. The Cattle Kingdom did more damage to the West than anything else in its economy of liquidation. As a mythology it will do even worse damage hereafter."[7]

### III  *"The West Against Itself"*

In "The West Against Itself" DeVoto expressed the belief that the cattle business of 1947 was dominated by the romance of the range cattle industry—the days of the open range (1870-86).[8] In the "Easy Chair" of the same month he wrote:

> The historian finds no convincing evidence that the cattle business was ever run intelligently enough to survive unassisted even in its great days, and is completely skeptical that it will ever be. Right now, with the sheep business co-operating, it is trying to make the cattle business impossible in the West within a generation. That, however, is not the greatest danger. For if the watersheds go, and they will go if cattlemen and sheepmen are allowed to get rid of government regulations of grazing, the West will go too—farms, ranches, towns, cities, irrigating systems, power plants, business in general. Much of the interior West will become uninhabitable, far more will be permanently depressed. The United States cannot afford to let that happen. You cannot afford to.
>
> While you are thinking about it, remember also that one of the pressures now urging cattlemen to destroy the range comes from the fact that they have, by their own official figures, at least fifteen million more cattle to graze than they ever had before. Those are the cattle which they have withheld from sale for the greater part of four years—from the sale to you and sometimes during the war from sale to the Army and Navy in which their sons were fighting. According to the Western press, action like this, when taken by a labor union, is a sitdown strike, inspired by Russia and encouraged by the New Deal. But when the sunburnt horseman does it, the Western press sees it as the protest of free men against interference with private enterprise by the bureaucrats and wildeyed theorists of Washington.[9]

In 1948 DeVoto, in an article making fun of the Western cowboy dress craze, said that, even where the cattle business was still "antiquated and anachronistic," as in the mountain states where "the cowboys" were trying to steal the public ranges to replace the land their stupid business methods had ruined, the "cowpoke" was merely a "dry-farmer mortgaged to the bank."[10]

In his first "Easy Chair" essay (1935), a defense of American individualism, DeVoto commented that during the preceding seventy years Congress had never guessed right about the Western lands then considered submarginal. He cited America's errors in the relocation of Indian tribes and indicated that some people might prefer living on submarginal lands—with their independence.[11]

While he disliked the government's interference with freedom in the attempts which were made to relocate people who were living on the submarginal lands, DeVoto liked what the government was doing toward reclamation of the land. In an article based on the Western trip he made in 1940 with Arthur M. Schlesinger, Jr., DeVoto wrote: "It is more heartening to see the progress that has been made against the forces of disintegration, forests growing in logged-out areas, dams holding water in midsummer that started downstream as a flood in late April, land being built up where land had been allowed to blow away. In such simplicities as these there is an assuagement hardly communicable in words, a palliative of our daily despair."[12]

Gradually, systematically, and logically, in the pages of *Harper's* DeVoto built up his case against the plunderers. In 1944 he wrote that more than a hundred million Americans needed to be told the facts of life about the West. These facts, he believed, were "that the natural resources of the West have been both ruthlessly and stupidly exploited, that they have mostly been exploited for the benefit of other sections, and that in consequence the plundered province has always been constructively bankrupt and sometimes actually bankrupt."

He believed that the state of Montana had been the worst offender of all the Western states. The vitriol flows freely through his analysis:

Throughout the West absentee ownership has channeled wealth out of the communities that produced it, but the system has reached its intolerable perfection in Montana. Throughout the West land and power and minerals have been cash crops, and unspeakable stupidity, waste, corruption, and cynicism have sometimes gone into the harvesting of them, but nowhere so intensively as in Montana. Elsewhere in the West there have been tragically unintelligent land use, destruction of vital wealth, contempt of human rights, purchase of men and obliteration of men who would not sell out, servile acceptance and futile rebellion, but all this has become most critical in Montana.[13]

In the tourist articles which were the result of the 1946 Western trip, as has been seen, DeVoto said little about the Plundered Province. The bitterness emerges only in short asides, such as his statement about private enterprise on the Missouri River, in which he says bluntly that a privately owned power company had several dams on the river and that it had not paid anything for the sites or for the people's water "which it used for power."[14]

In "The Anxious West," after an amusing analysis of the Western craze, he discussed the changes which had taken place since the 1940 trip, changes which were a result of the war. Westerners, he believed, thought that most of their troubles were the result of "colonial economic status and absentee control." The rich and the intellectuals of the West were unhappy about Western conditions; the rich, who were the representatives of absentee control, were not important—and intellectuals were the chief Western export! The chief trouble, DeVoto believed, was that the West had always encouraged conformity:

> Forever in rebellion against exterior exploitation, it has nevertheless always co-operated with the exploiters against itself when the chips were down. Worst of all, its own interior exploitation has always worked to the same end. No destruction by absentee-owned corporations of the West's natural resources—all it has—has ever been forestalled, because anything that could forestall it would also forestall the West's own destruction of those same resources. At this moment there is intended an assault on the public resources of the West which is altogether Western and so open that it cannot possibly be called a conspiracy. It is an assault which in a single generation could destroy the West and return it to the processes of geology. That such an intent publicly flourishes and may succeed—at the very moment the West is undertaking, with some possibility of success, to emancipate itself and establish an advanced industrial economy—is plain proof of schizophrenia.[15]

## IV   *The Schizophrenic West*

"The West Against Itself" analyzes fully this schizophrenia. The five economic forces which DeVoto believed were conspiring to destroy the free lands are almost the same as Turner's waves of settlement of the frontier. The West had undergone systematic exploitation, plundering, by these forces: (1) the fur trade, (2) mining, (3) the cattle business, (4) the oil business, and (5) the lumber industry. The fur trade, the mining industry, and the oil industry openly practiced a policy of depletion of natural resources; but the mining industry was the worst. Seemingly the miner's right to exploit transcended any other rights, for even the national government could not exercise effective control. The lumbermen, who owned much land in the West, also practiced a policy of total liquidation, but the national government had arrived on the scene in time to prevent complete destruction of the forests. Some of the big lumbermen practiced conservation, but the small operators did not.

DeVoto's chief target, however, was the cattlemen, who, he later insisted, were being used as a wedge to open the public lands to private exploitation and ownership. The cattle kings thought themselves free, but they were the peons of the Eastern bankers and of the railroads. They were in a continual struggle against the sheepmen and the farmers. And the cattle kingdom also was based on depletion, its success dependent on the use of free grazing land. In 1946 cattlemen were still grazing public lands at very low fees, actually acting as if they owned the land. The open range system, then, also involved liquidation, because overgrazing destroyed streams and caused erosion.

The New Deal, DeVoto said, had slowed the liquidation of natural resources. Then the Westerner had demanded more government help. The war had brought industry to the West, and in 1946 DeVoto believed that there was new hope for the area, except for the possibility of failure "inherent in its historic psychology." The Western schizophrenia, then, consisted of its desire for more help from the federal government and its fear of government control. The Western newspapers were afraid of communism and socialism; in effect they said to the federal government, "Get out, but give us more money."[16]

## V  The National Parks

In 1946 the chief attack of the exploiters was being made on the National Parks. DeVoto wrote:

The National Parks are composed of lands that were once part of the public domain (plus a few minute areas that had previously passed out of it). Exceedingly small in total area, they are permanently reserved and dedicated to their present uses: the preservation of wilderness areas, the protection of supreme scenic beauties, and the pleasure and recreation of the American people. By the terms of the original dedication and by policy so far kept inviolate they are to be maintained as they are, they are not to be commercially exploited at all. But they contain timber, grazing land, water, and minerals and that, in the West's eyes, is what is wrong with them.[17]

During World War II, attempts which were made to open the Sitka spruce forests in Olympia National Park to logging had failed—as did those to open them after the war to obtain lumber for veterans' homes. But DeVoto believed that more attempts would be made and that the West intended that the efforts be successful:

> The campaign had nothing to do with the Sitka spruce, winning the war, or housing veterans. Its purpose was to make a breach in the national parks policy with the aid of war emotions and to create a precedent. Once that precedent should be set, the rest would follow. Lumber companies could log the parks. Cattle and sheep associations could graze them. Mining companies could get at the mineral deposits. Power companies could build dams in them, water companies could use their lakes and rivers. Each of these objectives has been repeatedly attempted in the past and the sun never sets on the West's efforts to achieve them. Success would mean not only the destruction of the national parks but, as we shall see, far worse.[18]

DeVoto listed the forces which he believed were supporters of the attempted steal: the Western press, lumbermen, cattlemen and sheepmen, the mining industry, the United States Chamber of Commerce, certain Western congressmen, and the power companies. In 1946 the stockmen and wool-growers were doing the agitating, demanding (1) self-regulation, (2) the sale of grazing land to themselves, and (3) the reclassification and sale of Forest Service controlled grazing lands to private interests. The ultimate goal, DeVoto believed, was the elimination of all public ownership of grazing and forest lands.

DeVoto named the Western congressional leaders who were

continually introducing grazing bills into the Senate and the House. The process involved in the conspiracy, he said, was to get the public lands transferred to the individual states, which were controlled by big business. Then the state lands were to be transferred to private ownership. This connivance, DeVoto believed, would result in the destruction of all Western public lands; but "to a historian it has the beauty of any historical continuity. It is the Western psychology working within the pattern which its own nature set. It is the forever recurrent lust to liquidate the West that is so large a part of Western history. The West has always been a society living under threat of destruction by natural cataclysm and here it is, bright against the sky, inviting such cataclysm."[19]

DeVoto insisted that the life of the nation depended on the proper use of the land. In the "Easy Chair" essay published in the same issue of *Harper's* as "The West Against Itself," he insisted that ancient civilizations had died because of misuse of the land, because the soil was denuded of its forests and grasses. Ancient Mesopotamia and modern Spain were used as examples. What happened to Spain between 1200 and 1600, he believed, was typical of twentieth century practices in the United States. The land was overgrazed; it was so poor by 1600 that a drastic reduction of the herds had to be made, and Spanish agriculture never overcame this handicap. Thus deforestation and overgrazing were the causes of the economic collapse of Spain in the seventeenth century.

In the twentieth century, overgrazing in the Wasatch area of Utah damaged the economy of the state. The government with the Civilian Conservation Corps got on the job there too late. The cause of the Utah difficulty, according to DeVoto, was unrestricted overgrazing. His conclusion was that, if the governmental lands were thrown open to unrestricted grazing, the resources of the West would be destroyed.[20]

In the June, 1947, issue of *Harper's* DeVoto described the reaction the January articles. Certain sheepgrowers wrote to the Western newspapers attacking the editors of *Harper's* as "Communistic New Dealers"—but they at the same time opposed and stopped proposals made in Congress to do away with government regulations which artificially controlled the price of wool. DeVoto insisted again that the United States Chamber of Commerce, the cattlemen, and the sheepmen were in league to amend the Taylor Act which restricted grazing; that they were trying to gain control of Western grazing lands, even those in the national forests; and that other interests, already named, were trying to gain control of all of the public resources of the West. This land grab was not succeeding, however, because the small ranches and some Western politicians had begun to oppose it. The Idaho legislature had in March repeated in a memorial to Congress DeVoto's ideas which had appeared in the January issue of *Harper's*. The battle was now in the open. DeVoto concluded:

> The ultimate objectives of the biggest land grab in our history are to extinguish the public interest in all lands now held by the government that can be used by cattle, sheep, mining, lumber, or power companies. The immediate objectives of the joint committee are to get the publicly-held grazing lands into private ownership and to add to that monopoly all portions of the national forests that can be grazed. A good many Westerners have begun to protest to their congressmen. Wherever you live, your interests and those of your grandchildren are endangered. You, too, have representatives in Congress and a stamp.[21]

A year after the January, 1947, attack, DeVoto again reviewed the facts about the Western land grab; and this time he plainly stated what he believed would happen if the land grab worked. He gave what he believed were four facts about the Western land grab:

> One: the first objective is to get into state ownership as a step toward private ownership, or into private ownership directly, all publicly owned grazing lands; success would mean the destruction of the fundamental Western watersheds. Two: the ultimate objective is the conversion to private ownership of all the public lands in ten Western states; this would mean the end of conservation in the United States and, within a generation, the destruction of the intermountain West. Three: the drive is spearheaded by the national associations of cattlegrowers and wool-growers, is conducted in the interests of a relatively few large-scale operators, is clearly detrimental to the interests of cattlemen and sheepmen in general, is being vigorously opposed by an increasing number of them and by other Westerners. Four: invisible so far behind the spearhead are other, more powerful inter-

ests which will profit enormously if the public lands pass into private ownership or private control, if conservation practices are stopped or even weakened, if the precedents are broken, or if governmental regulations can be ended or even reduced.

In the same essay he cited a rigged committee meeting (a subcommittee of the House Committee on Public Lands) which tried to discredit the Forest Service and to weaken it by reducing its appropriation as evidence that the conspiracy was a real one.[22]

## VI  *Party Politics and the Western Lands*

Until May, 1948, DeVoto kept partisan politics out of his discussion of the Western land grab, but in his "Easy Chair" essay of that month he began to talk about national parties and conservation. It is not necessary here to discuss DeVoto's politics in detail; this has already been done in Arthur M. Schlesinger's essay in *Four Portraits and One Subject*. DeVoto's thinking was independent of partisan ideas. In the May essay, which is an encomium of Gifford Pinchot's *Breaking New Ground*, he wrote that Pinchot made conservation of natural resources a national policy and tried to make it a world policy. From this evaluation he progressed to praise of President Theodore Roosevelt, a Republican, who, he said, would always be honored as a conservationist:

It is an exciting and profoundly heartening spectacle: T.R. and Pinchot and their brilliant aides pitchforking from the public service the manure of the golden calf, cleaning out the graft that generations had made so functional in the General Land Office that history calls it our worst administrative corruption, making headway against the corruption in the Indian Service that was even older and almost as complete, halting and prosecuting timber thieves and coal thieves, halting large-scale corporate violations of the homestead laws, withdrawing from the possibility of exploitation by private monopoly irrigation sites and power sites and forests and grazing lands and fundamental watersheds. The spectacle, in short, of the establishment as a policy to which the United States was committed of conserving the publicly owned natural resources of the United States for public use and for the benefit of the public—in perpetuity.

[ 122 ]

DeVoto noted that this conservation program was begun by Republicans. When another Republican, William Howard Taft, attempted to impede conservation, he split the Republican party. In 1948, DeVoto wrote, the assault against the public lands was led by the Republican party; the Republican on the national level, he said, who called for reform of the public lands policy was Harold Stassen.[23]

Already, in his analysis of the election of 1940, DeVoto had traced the histories of the two parties and had said that in 1800, 1828, 1884, 1912, and 1932, the Democratic party had come to power "charged with the duty of repairing situations and arresting trends which had carried the nation dangerously out of equilibrium." Each time virtually a revolution was accomplished; each time the abuses rectified by the Democratic party were "primarily those associated with concentrations of economic or financial power." This financial power, DeVoto evidently believed, underlay the Western land grab.[24]

So DeVoto began to single out Republican politicians and to reveal their part in attempting to steal the public lands. In July, 1948, he summarized the content of previous essays to proclaim again that the current plea of "returning the public lands to the states" was a red herring. For the most part, the Western public lands had never been owned by the states. He cited as stupid the statement by one of the Congressional leaders that overgrazing had no adverse effect: "Erosion has always been with us." He concluded: "If the West cannot control the exceedingly small number of people whose program would destroy it, the rest of the country will have to control them for the West's sake and its own."[25]

In the same issue of *Harper's*, in a special article entitled "Sacred Cows and Public Lands," DeVoto summarized what he had said before in the "Easy Chair." He raised the question of why there was so much fuss about "returning the public lands to state control" since only two percent of grazing land for cattle and seven percent for sheep were involved. The answer, he said, was that the pressure group was interested in "undermining all federal authority over any part of the public lands." He also noted that an opponent of conservation had implied that "to protect the ranges, the forests, and the watersheds is communism."

DeVoto noted with glee that this statement and other attempts to gain control of the public lands had backfired, that opposition had become too strong. He warned again that attacks on the Forest Service were part of an unceasing attempt to discredit all attempts at conservation and that unexploited natural resources should be guarded carefully against the powerful economic interests.[26] In the March, 1949, "Easy Chair," DeVoto made an extended plea for more money for the National Park Service, which was responsible for protection of the parks.

DeVoto continued to watch and to report attempts to return the public lands to state control. In the March, 1951, "Easy Chair" he again described the issues and suggested that the grazing fees on public lands be the same as those on privately owned lands. He noted that a new bill to put grazing rights under state control had been proposed and asked the public to be on watch.[27]

Then, in October, 1952, DeVoto analyzed in detail a plank in the Republican platform, included by General Pat Hurley at the behest of the stockgrowers, that was an attack on the Forest Service. DeVoto pointed out that the use of the forest lands for grazing by stockmen was in effect a subsidy by American taxpayers. When the Republican platform spoke of the "traditional public lands policy," DeVoto asked, what policy did it refer to? Theodore Roosevelt, a Republican, was a conservationist. There were other Republican policies also: Secretary Richard A. Ballinger sought to turn public coal and timber lands over to private owners; Secretary A. B. Fall tried to turn public oil lands over to private operators; other Republicans had tried to turn grazing lands over to private owners. Just which Republican policy did the platform refer to?

The platform asked for "opportunity for ownership by citizens to promote the highest land use" and for elimination "of arbitrary bureaucratic practices." It sought to protect the public against "monopolistic exploitation and bureaucratic favoritism." DeVoto pointed out that the public lands plank in the platform embodied a bill that had been worked up early in 1952 as an attack on the Forest Service and then was not approved by Congress. The bill favored a minority of stockgrowers, the big operators and manipulators. And then DeVoto rewrote the public land plank:

We pledge the Republican Party to strip the Forest Service of its power to regulate and administer its grazing ranges, and to transfer that power to the present holders of grazing permits. We favor legislation which will put grazing, a subsidiary use of national forests and in dollars the least important one, in a position superior and adverse to other uses such as lumbering, mining, irrigation, municipal and industrial water supply, watershed protection, hunting, fishing, camping, and the public interest in general. We demand that there be no protection of ranges or watersheds by reducing the number of stock now permitted to graze them or by any change we do not like in the terms on which grazing permits are held. We also demand an Act of Congress that will give the present holders of grazing permits a legally vested hold on the national forests, will enable them to keep other stockmen out of the forests, will authorize them to set grazing fees as they see fit, and will empower them to formulate and enforce their own regulations without regard to the public interest.

The plank, DeVoto believed, represented a minority of the seventeen thousand stockmen who held grazing permits and ignored the rights of the rest of the American people.[28]

## VII  *State Versus Federal Control*

In February, 1953, the "Easy Chair" directed arguments against "returning" the public lands at the Wyoming Farm Bureau Federation. Among other things, DeVoto showed that the states were unable to regulate and operate the parks. He predicted that attempts would again be made to scuttle the Forest Service:

When it begins, Congress should remember three things: that the public lands belong to the citizens of forty-eight states and not to 2 percent of eleven, that impairment of the public lands would arrest progress in the West and ultimately make the region a charge on the rest of the country, and that the public lands are the only responsibility of the government besides atomic energy about which Congress could make an irretrievable mistake, one that could not be corrected later on. For if the public lands are once relinquished, or even if any fundamental change is made in the present system, they will be gone for good.[29]

In the May issue of the same year DeVoto described the fraud that had been practiced in carrying out the Timber and Stone

Act, as well as other activities which he considered harmful to the national interests. DeVoto's summary is typical: "The redwood forests deals, the Oregon timber frauds, Teapot Dome—they were peanuts, birdseed, compared to what this crew of bluesky pitchmen are asking Congress to slip over on us now. But the stench still rises from them and drifts down history and over Capitol Hill. Congress will sit this one out, the carefully planned agenda notwithstanding."[30]

Again in July, in a review of a United States Chamber of Commerce radio program entitled "The Public Lands," DeVoto reiterated his opposition to the Land Grab. In October of the same year he made an impassioned plea for more money for the National Park Service. In the August, 1954, issue of *Harper's* he published an article entitled "Conservation Down and on the Way Out," a summary of the controversy in which he accuses the Eisenhower administration of giving in to "the cowboys." (This article, like some of the others, was reprinted in *The Easy Chair.*)

Then, on the "Easy Chair" of November of the same year, DeVoto digressed an article filled with optimism:

(A lot of people have written to me asking what happened to the Hope-Aiken grazing bill and the bill to authorize Echo Park Dam. Both of them died in the closing days of the session. Though that verb is technically accurate, in actual fact both were killed: the opposition licked them. It may well be that the grazing bill is licked for good. The forces lined up behind the Hope-Aiken bill were not enough to pass it and they were greater, it seems likely, than any that can again be mobilized in support of its objectives.)[31]

Two months later, after the election of 1954, he predicted that the Echo Park Dam Project, though approved by Eisenhower, would not be approved (the dam was to cover the Dinosaur Monument). After noting that certain anticonservationists had been defeated in the election of 1954, DeVoto wrote: "We may reasonably expect that the forays against the national forests by the cowboys and the trade associations of the lumber manufacturers will be stopped even colder than they have been up to now, that the Bureau of Reclamation will be kept out of Dinosaur Monument, and that a half dozen other raids on national parks will get nowhere."

In the same essay DeVoto gave what was very nearly his last word on the subject. Later he wrote again against the Echo Park Dam project and against advertising which condemned the public parks system. In September, 1955, he argued for more national and state parks. But the advice given in the "Easy Chair" of January, 1955, is a good last word on the subject:

> Again, there should be a strenuous counterattack on the foolish allegations that REA, TVA, and the public power program are "socialistic." These are no more socialistic than the Post Office Department or a church supper. On the strictest theory of classic capitalism they are capitalistic instruments, far more so than the private collectivism of the holding companies, as conveniently illustrated by Dixon-Yates. Finally, if it is desirable to have the federal government generate 15 per cent of our electric power, instead of the 10 per cent it now generates, or to have what the Chamber of Commerce calls "a land-hungry bureaucracy" buy up another million acres of cut-over and eroding timberland in the East and South, there is no reason to be defensive. Add such measures to the program and start fighting for them.[32]

# Writer and Man

THE PROBLEM that has continually plagued regional American literature, especially Western and Southwestern literature, is twofold. First, regional writers tend merely to glorify the regional; their literature is temporal, shallow, parochial. Second, great numbers of writers leave their native regions and emigrate to the literary centers, where, for economic security, they write popular literature inferior to their original art.

Many examples of the merely regional writers can be found among the local colorists of the period just after the Civil War: Mary Noailles Murfree, John Fox, Jr., Mary E. Wilkins Freeman, Sarah Orne Jewett, Bret Harte, and others. The merely regional, being limited in time and space, quite obviously lacks the universality that one associates with great literature. The regionalists who have been more successful have somehow transcended the limitations of setting and have produced great literature. William Faulkner and Thomas Wolfe might be considered as examples of such writers.

A well-known example of a writer who began by writing substantial, realistic fiction and eventually became a creator of slick potboilers is Hamlin Garland, who could have fulfilled the promise of *Main-Travelled Roads, Rose of Dutcher's Coolly,* and *Crumbling Idols* by becoming a leader of a new realistic frontier literature but instead contributed such works as *The Captain of the Gray Horse Troop* and *Cavanaugh, Forest Ranger* to the literary world. Even Howells did not remain completely independent; his work as an editor, however, helped him to preserve his literary integrity. Thus, those who left their native regions and have managed to write accurately and realistically of the land left behind are rare. A list of those who showed unfulfilled promise should include George Sessions Perry, Edwin Lanham, Sigman Byrd, Oliver La Farge, and others.

Bernard DeVoto was, I believe, one of those rare persons who left the West and emigrated to the Eastern literary centers but retained a clear-sighted interest in the Western region. He left the West to teach at Northwestern University; he left Northwestern to move to Cambridge, where he thought he could do better work. He taught at Harvard University, and he did editorial work. Basically, however, he was a free-lance writer; without apology, he wrote for money. And in his works there was always a consistency of attitude toward Western America, about which he tried to present the truth.

DeVoto's writing was limited and at the same time strengthened by his insistence on facts. His picture of the frontiersman was not influenced by the romanticizing of numerous novelists and historians about the pioneer; to DeVoto the frontiersmen were men of ordinary stature. On the other hand, he did not subscribe to the concept of the frontiersman as a mean, skulking scoundrel, a description set forth by Eastern and English visitors (who were gulled by the frontiersmen themselves) and reiterated by Van Wyck Brooks and others. DeVoto again insisted that the facts be considered, that the men on the frontier were neither demigods nor monsters.

DeVoto's histories afford ample factual evidence that the westering Americans were ordinary people with extraordinary curiosity; that they were interesting individuals, not types. In *Year of Decision* and *Across the Wide Missouri,* especially, DeVoto made full analyses of many different individuals. And the same strong-minded attitude toward finding the facts and nailing them down caused him to view America's westward expansion with unusual clarity.

On such controversial questions as the moral justification of the Mexican War, he makes no judgment; he just presents the facts. He does show, however, that the idea of Manifest Destiny was so strong in America in the 1840's that not even Presidents could resist it—a fact that we must accept as such. DeVoto insists that the "War Between the States" was in fact a Civil War, and that the nation's rights taking precedence over those of the states is a fact established by that war.

DeVoto's love for fact led him to disagree violently with those who pictured Mark Twain as a shrinking violet afraid of his Western environment. The same love of fact caused his violent controversy with critics who pictured the America of the 1920's and 1930's as an empty wasteland. He also maintained that the major writers of the period, the Lost Generation writers, did not give an accurate or adequate picture of America. He preferred Frost to Eliot, Robinson to Pound, Twain and Howells to Henry James.

This method—and it was a consistent one—led DeVoto in his "Easy Chair" essays to defend America against its detractors, to show that American civilization was not as hopelessly sordid as its critics insisted. It caused him to oppose those who attacked American free enterprise during the tumultuous period before World War II, while at the same time he predicted the coming of that war several years in advance.

At the same time that he defended American civilization, which he felt to be based on both American individualism and cooperation, he made sarcastic attacks on the products of American free enterprise. His pleas for better automobiles and especially better automobile tires were numerous. His antipathy towards "stainless steel" and his pleas for better household knives were constant. And, when the time came for him to take a stand against private enterprise and for governmental control of the public grazing lands, forest lands, and park areas, he did so without hesitation.

DeVoto used his vast knowledge of Western history to bolster his attacks on the forces which were plundering the West. His being a Westerner did not keep him from presenting the facts and drawing conclusions from them. Almost incidentally he described in detail the professional Westerner, with his Madison Avenue Western garb and his hat patterned on those worn originally by Yankee swine herders, and he devastatingly revealed the emptiness of the picture. Calmly he showed the absurdity of the romantic picture of the cowboy—still exploited by the movies, by television, and by historians with imaginary saddle burns—by showing the lack of reason and the downright criminal destructiveness of the cattle kingdom, which exploited and virtually destroyed the grazing lands of the West.

While his attacks on the exploiters of Western lands and natural resources made DeVoto unpopular with the newspapers, the politicians, and some of the people of the West, anyone reading his articles can see a consistent viewpoint, backed up by his understanding of the forces at work in the West. His love of the West was real; his dislike of those who could not perceive that the West had always suffered at the hands of Eastern capitalists—and because of the nearsightedness of Westerners—was bitter. The same balance between his love of the West and his dislike of its detractors and exploiters is apparent in DeVoto's writing, from *The Crooked Mile* (1924), his early reviews of Western books, and his article on Utah in the *American Mercury* of 1926 to the last articles in *Harper's*.

In order to get a full picture of DeVoto, the man, one would need to study carefully his letters and other yet unpublished documents. The numerous tributes written to him at the time of his death do not present a full picture. Essays by personal friends—Catherine Drinker Bowen, Edith R. Mirrielees, Arthur M. Schlesinger, Jr., and Wallace Stegner—in *Four Portraits and One Subject: Bernard DeVoto* give insights into his character. The article by Schlesinger, it seems to me, reveals more about DeVoto than do the other three; moreover, the errors in fact of the other three essays would annoy DeVoto.

One can, however, make some generalizations about the man simply on the basis of what he has written. His hatred of sham and his iconoclastic attacks on representatives of the status quo invite comparison with Mencken, although DeVoto's kindliness is more apparent. His devotion to the facts and his determination to go where facts led him and no further are consistently apparent in his writing. In his writings about the West and, in fact, in all of his works, DeVoto's ideas were always based on the solid foundation of knowledge. The amount of research and reading which went into the writing of the histories must have been great. It is true that he wrote histories which covered much territory and time, but at the same time they were based on minute details. Moreover, his love of verbal combat and his persistence when he thought he was right seem typical of his character. All of this was tempered by breadth of vision, depth of understanding, and a ready wit.

It has not yet been fully determined what DeVoto's place is in the literature of the twentieth century, but it is apparent that few saw as clearly as he did the importance of the American frontier and its continuing impact on American civilization. His evaluation of the Western complex—past, present, and future—is unique in American writing, for it is neither rosily romantic nor inanely iconoclastic.

# Notes and References

## Chapter One

1. "The Citizen," in *Four Portraits and One Subject: Bernard DeVoto* (Boston, 1963), p. 41.
2. *Ibid., passim.*
3. Julius P. Barclay, "A Bibliography of the Writing of Bernard DeVoto," in *ibid.*, pp. 117ff. Robert Edson Lee, in "The Work of Bernard DeVoto, Introduction and Annotated Checklist" (Doctoral dissertation, State University of Iowa, 1957), *ibid.*, p. 131, states that DeVoto did the chapter on diction. That chapter, to me, seems modern (and sensible).
4. *The House of Sun-Goes-Down* (New York, 1928), p. 94.
5. *Ibid.*, p. 98.
6. *The Crooked Mile* (New York, 1924), pp. 309-10.
7. *Ibid.*, p. 327.
8. *Ibid.*, p. 150.
9. *Ibid.*, p. 149.
10. *Ibid.*, p. 145.
11. *The Chariot of Fire* (New York, 1926), pp. 8-9.
12. *Ibid.*, p. 20.
13. *Ibid.*, p. 27.
14. *Ibid.*, pp. 46-47.
15. *The Crooked Mile*, p. 23.
16. *Ibid.*, p. 33.
17. *Ibid.*, p. 34.
18. *Ibid.*, pp. 141-42.
19. *Ibid.*, p. 211.
20. *Ibid.*, pp. 274-75.
21. *Four Portraits and One Subject: Bernard DeVoto*, pp. 100-101.
22. *Minority Report* (Boston, 1940), p. 175.
23. *Forays and Rebuttals* (Boston, 1936), p. vii.

## Chapter Two

1. *Mark Twain's America* (Boston, 1932), p. 41 n.
2. "Brave Days in Washoe," *American Mercury*, XVII (June, 1929), 228-37; "The Real Frontier: a Preface to Mark Twain," *Harper's Magazine*, CLXIII (June, 1931), 60-71; "The Matrix of Mark

Twain's Humour," *The Boookman,* LXXIV (October, 1931), 172-78; "Mark Twain and the Genteel Tradition," *The Harvard Graduates' Magazine,* XL (December, 1931), 155-63. Perhaps others were published, but these are the principal articles.

3. *Mark Twain's America,* p. ix.
4. *Ibid.*
5. *Ibid.,* p. 41 n.
6. *The Portable Mark Twain* (New York, 1946), p. 30.
7. *Mark Twain's America,* pp. ix-xi.
8. *Ibid.,* pp. xii-xiii.
9. *Minority Report,* pp. 187-88.
10. *Ibid.,* p. 176.
11. *Ibid.,* p. 236.
12. *Forays and Rebuttals,* pp. 172-73.
13. *Mark Twain's America,* p. 225.
14. *Ibid.,* pp. 27-29.
15. *Ibid.,* pp. 32-34.
16. *Ibid.,* pp. 35-39.
17. Cited in *Ibid.,* p. 41.
18. *Ibid.,* p. 42.
19. *Ibid.,* p. 53-54.
20. *Ibid.,* pp. 55ff.
21. *Ibid.,* pp. 90-91.
22. *Ibid.,* pp. 100ff. The quotation is from pp. 132-33.
23. *Ibid.,* p. 175.
24. *Ibid.,* pp. 206–7.
25. *Ibid.,* pp. 218-23.
26. *Ibid.,* pp. 223-31.
27. *Ibid.,* p. 257.
28. *Ibid.,* p. 260.
29. *Ibid.,* p. 308.
30. *Forays and Rebuttals,* pp. 348-72.
31. *Ibid.,* pp. 359-60.
32. *Ibid.,* p. 372.
33. *Ibid.,* pp. 373-403. As far as I have been able to tell, this essay and "Mark Twain: The Ink of History" are available only in *Forays and Rebuttals,* now long out of print. The centennial essay is DeVoto's most important essay on Twain; the MLA essay is a devastating attack on literary critics. Its importance will be shown later.
34. *Ibid.,* pp. 391, 402.
35. *Mark Twain at Work* (Cambridge, 1942), p. vii.
36. *Ibid.,* pp. vii-viii.
37. *Ibid.,* pp. 23–24.
38. *Ibid.,* p. 88.

39. *Ibid.*, p. 100.
40. *Ibid.*, pp. 102-3.

## Chapter Three

1. *Forays and Rebuttals*, p. vii.
2. *Ibid.*, pp. 163-65.
3. *Ibid.*, pp. 181–82.
4. *The World of Fiction* (Boston, 1950), pp. xi-xii.
5. *Forays and Rebuttals*, p. 374.
6. *Ibid.*, pp. 373-74.
7. *Ibid.*, pp. 374-76. This summary, of necessity, leaves out much of the wit and wisdom of DeVoto's examples. The first two kinds of criticism he calls "sub-basements" and the third the "main basement." His paragraph on the "obscene activity" of American scholars in analyzing the influences on Poe (381) is amusing to one who shares DeVoto's opinion of Poe.
8. *Ibid.*, p. 378.
9. *Ibid.*, pp. 390–92.
10. *Ibid.*, p. 385.
11. *Ibid.*, p. 388.
12. *Ibid.*, pp. 396-401.
13. *Ibid.*, p. 402.
14. *Ibid.*, pp. 402-3.
15. *Minority Report*, pp. 144-45.
16. *Ibid.*, pp. 14-49.
17. *Ibid.*, p. 149.
18. Edmund Wilson, "Complaints: II, Bernard DeVoto," *New Republic*, LXXXIX (February 3, 1937), 406.
19. *Minority Report*, pp. 164-65.
20. *The Literary Fallacy* (Boston, 1944), p. 4.
21. *Ibid.*, p. 5.
22. *Ibid.*, pp. 7, 15, 17, 18, 22.
23. *Ibid.*, pp. 24-28.
24. *Ibid.*, pp. 29-32.
25. *Ibid.*, pp. 31, 50.
26. *Ibid.*, pp. 33-38. The notes on the second chapter, "Oh, Lost America," are excellent. On p. 52, n. 8, DeVoto analyzed the "eidolon" of Puritanism, showed that Mencken and others had confused Puritanism with the doctrines of the evangelical sects, and concluded: "Puritanism was just something to which you attributed whatever portions of our culture you happened to dislike." Critics still follow this practice.
27. *Ibid.*, pp. 38-39.
28. *Ibid.*, pp. 39-43.

29. *Ibid.,* pp. 57-58.

30. *Ibid.,* pp. 62-75.

31. *Ibid.,* pp. 75-88.

32. Chapter IV is pp. 95-123 of the volume. My conclusions are drawn from the last few pages.

33. *Ibid.,* p. 135. The summary is of pp. 124-35.

34. *Ibid.,* p. 150.

35. *Ibid.,* pp. 172-75. The summary is of pp. 151-72.


## Chapter Four

1. "What's the Matter with History?," *Harper's Magazine,* CLXXIX (June, 1939), 109-12.

2. *Mark Twain's America,* p. ix.

3. See Julius P. Barclay's bibliography in *Four Portraits and One Subject: Bernard DeVoto.*

4. *Ibid.,* pp. 131-32.

5. *Ibid.,* pp. 108, 130.

6. *The Year of Decision, 1846* (Boston, 1943), p. 496.

7. *Ibid.,* p. 517.

8. *Ibid.,* p. x.

9. "The Easy Chair," *Harper's Magazine,* CLXXXVII (July, 1943), 129-32. (From January, 1943 through September, 1949, "The Easy Chair" was the only title in *Harper's.*)

10. *Ibid.,* p. 115.

11. *Mark Twain's America,* pp. 3, 331.

12. *The Year of Decision,* p. 3.

13. *Ibid.,* pp. 3-4.

14. *Ibid.,* pp. 7-8.

15. *Ibid.,* pp. 8–9. The phrase "Manifest Destiny" was first used in the July-August, 1845, issue of the *U.S. Magazine and Democratic Review.* The anonymous author of the essay may have been John L. O'Sullivan. See Drake DeKay, "Manifest Destiny," *Encyclopedia Americana* (1964), XVIII, 218d.

16. *Ibid.,* pp. 9-10.

17. *Ibid.,* p. 139.

18. *Ibid.*

19. *Ibid.,* pp. 292-93.

20. *Ibid.,* p. 138.

21. *Ibid.,* pp. 359-60.

22. *Ibid.,* p. 191.

23. *Ibid.,* p. 403.

24. *Across the Wide Missouri* (Boston, 1947), p. xi.

25. *Ibid.,* p. xii.

26. *Ibid.*, p. 247.

27. *Ibid.*, pp. 248-49.

28. *Ibid.*, pp. 200-203.

29. *Ibid.*, p. 203.

30. *Ibid.*, pp. 232, 371-72, 354-55, 378-79.

31. *Ibid.*, p. 298.

32. *Ibid.*, pp. 300-301.

33. "The Easy Chair," *Harper's Magazine*, CXCVIII (April, 1949), 53, 55.

34. *The Course of Empire* (Boston, 1952), p. xiv.

35. *Ibid.*

36. *Ibid.*, p. xv.

37. *Ibid.*, pp. 400-402.

38. *Ibid.*, p. 403.

39. *The Louisiana Purchase* (Springfield, Ohio, 1953), pp. 9, 14. Originally published as "Celebrating 150 Years of the Louisiana Purchase," *Collier's*, CXXI (March 21, 1953), 44-50†.

40. *Ibid.*, pp. 34-36, 68-73, 191, 373-79, 470-71, *passim*. The index is a gold mine.

41. *The Course of Empire*, pp. 93, 174, 209, 238, *passim*.

42. "The Visual Instrument," *Harper's Magazine*, CCVI (June, 1953), 52.

43. *The Journals of Lewis and Clark* (Boston, 1953), pp. v-vi.

44. *Ibid.*, p. lii.

## Chapter Five

1. "The Easy Chair," *Harper's Magazine*, CXCI (November, 1945), 410-12. Since during the twenty years DeVoto wrote the "Easy Chair" the format changed several times, for convenience and consistency the "Easy Chair" essays will be cited in an abbreviated form for this chapter and Chapter Six. Full citations will be made for *Harper's* articles other than "Easy Chair" essays.

2. *Ibid.*, 413.

3. *Harper's*, CLXXIV (December, 1936), 112.

4. *Harper's*, CLXXXI (December, 1940), 110.

5. *Harper's*, CLXXXVII (February, 1944), 245.

6. "The Anxious West," *Harper's Magazine*, CXCIII (December, 1946), 480.

7. *Harper's*, CLXXXI (December, 1940), 111–12.

8. *Harper's*, CLXXVII (September, 1938), 447-48.

9. *Ibid.*, 448.

10. *Harper's*, CLXXXIII (October, 1941), 445.

11. *Harper's*, CLXXXVI (December, 1942), 109-12.

12. *Harper's,* CLXXXVI (March, 1943), 437-40.
13. *Harper's,* CLXXXVIII (April, 1944), 426-27.
14. *Harper's,* CXC (December, 1944), 35.
15. *Harper's,* CLXXX (February, 1940), 336.
16. *Harper's,* CLXXXVII (September, 1943), 338-40.
17. *Harper's,* CLXXVI (December, 1937), 109-10.
18. *Harper's,* CLXXII (December, 1935), 126-28.
19. *Harper's,* CLXXIV (February, 1937), 333.
20. *Harper's,* CLXXXII (February, 1941), 445-48.
21. *Harper's,* CLXXXII (April, 1941), 560.
22. *Harper's,* CLXXII (January, 1936), 253-56.
23. *Harper's,* CLXXVI (May, 1938), 669-72.
24. *Harper's,* CCI (November, 1950), 67.

### Chapter Six

1. "The West: a Plundered Province," *Harper's Magazine,* CLXXIX (August, 1934), 335-64.
2. *Harper's,* CCXI (November, 1955), 10. As in Chapter Five, citations to "Easy Chair" essays are abbreviated.
3. See *Harper's,* CCIX (November, 1954), 14, and CCX (January, 1955), 15.
4. "The Citizen," in *Four Portraits and One Subject: Bernard DeVoto* (Boston, 1963), pp. 74-75.
5. *Harper's,* CXCVII (October, 1948), 89.
6. *Harper's,* CXXXVIII (February, 1944), 244.
7. "The Anxious West," *Harper's Magazine,* CXCIII (December, 1946), 482, 485.
8. "The West Against Itself," *Harper's Magazine,* CXCIV (January, 1947), 3.
9. *Harper's,* CXCIV (January, 1947), 48.
10. *Harper's,* CXCVII (November, 1948), 59.
11. *Harper's,* CLXXI (November, 1935), 767.
12. "Main Street Twenty Years After," *Harper's Magazine,* CLXXXI (November, 1940), 587.
13. *Harper's,* CLXXXVIII (February, 1944), 243.
14. *Harper's,* CXCIII (August, 1946), 129.
15. "The Anxious West," *Harper's Magazine,* CXCIII (December, 1946), 481-86, 489-91.
16. "The West Against Itself," *Harper's Magazine,* CXCIV (January, 1947), 1-7. The first half of the article is here summarized. The entire essay appears in *The Easy Chair,* pp. 231-56.
17. *Ibid.,* p. 9.
18. *Ibid.*

19. *Ibid.*, pp. 10-13.

20. *Harper's,* CXCIV (January, 1947), 46-47.

21. *Harper's,* CXCIV (June, 1947), 543-46.

22. *Harper's,* CXCVI (January, 1948), 28-31.

23. *Harper's,* CXCVI (May, 1948), 441-44.

24. *Harper's,* CLXXXII (January, 1941), 221-22.

25. *Harper's,* CXCVII (July, 1948), 108-12. Reprinted as "Statesmen on the Lam," *The Easy Chair,* pp. 283-91.

26. "Sacred Cows and Public Lands," *Harper's Magazine,* CXCVII (July, 1948), 46-55. Entire essay reprinted in *The Easy Chair,* pp. 257-82.

27. *Harper's,* CCII (March, 1951), 48–51. Reprinted in *The Easy Chair,* pp. 293-300.

28. *Harper's,* CCV (October, 1952), 65-68.

29. *Harper's,* CCVI (February, 1953), 56. Essay reprinted in *The Easy Chair,* pp. 301-9.

30. *Harper's,* CCVI (May, 1953), 57-60. Reprinted in *The Easy Chair,* pp. 311-19.

31. *Harper's,* CCIX (November, 1954), 14.

32. *Harper's,* CCX (January, 1955), 12-15.

# Selected Bibliography

Despite the position Bernard DeVoto occupied in American letters, remarkably little has been written about him. My purpose has not been to assemble a complete bibliography; a fairly complete bibliographical study is in print (see the last item in this list). This work has utilized primary sources, not secondary sources, because the secondary sources are negligible. I have made no attempt to compile a full bibliography of the critical controversy surrounding the publication of *The Literary Fallacy*.

## PRIMARY SOURCES

### 1. *Books by Bernard DeVoto*

*Across the Wide Missouri*. Boston: Houghton Mifflin Company, 1947. Literary interpretation of the history of the Rocky Mountain fur trade; illustrated with paintings by Alfred Jacob Miller and Charles Bodmer.

*The Chariot of Fire*. New York: The Macmillan Company, 1926. Novel about Ohio Boggs, frontiersman, who finally convinced himself that he was God.

*The Course of Empire*. Boston: Houghton Mifflin Company, 1952. Panoramic history of America from the coming of the first white man to the arrival of the Lewis and Clark expedition at the Pacific Ocean.

*The Crooked Mile*. New York: Minton, Balch, and Company, 1924. Novel about the younger generation of the pioneer Abbey family; contains the fictional historian John Gale's theories about the frontier.

*The Easy Chair*. Boston: Houghton Mifflin Company, 1955. Collection of "Easy Chair" essays.

*Forays and Rebuttals*. Boston: Little, Brown, and Company, 1936. Early collection of essays by DeVoto on many subjects.

*The Hour*. Boston: Houghton Mifflin Company, 1951. Rewriting of three essays on drinking.

*The House of Sun-Goes-Down*. New York: The Macmillan Company, 1928. Novel about life of James Abbey, patriarch of the Abbey family.

*The Literary Fallacy*. Boston: Little, Brown, and Company, 1944. DeVoto's clearest, most concise statement of the basis of his running argument with Van Wyck Brooks and his followers.

*The Louisiana Purchase.* Springfield, Ohio: Crowell-Collier, 1953. Illustrated pamphlet, originally published as "Celebrating 150 Years of the Louisiana Purchase," *Collier's,* CXXI (March 21, 1953), 44-50†.

*Mark Twain at Work.* Cambridge: Harvard University Press, 1942. Collection of three Mark Twain essays, one a University of Chicago lecture and the others introductions to the Limited Editions Club's *Tom Sawyer* and *Huckleberry Finn.*

*Mark Twain's America.* Boston: Little, Brown, and Company, 1932. Important work about Mark Twain; classified as history, social history, literary theory, and criticism.

*Minority Report.* Boston: Little, Brown, and Company, 1940. DeVoto's second collection of essays on many subjects.

*Mountain Time.* Boston: Little, Brown, and Company, 1947. DeVoto's last and most popular novel; deals with the conflict between the ideals of the East and the Mountain West.

*We Accept with Pleasure.* Boston: Little, Brown, and Company, 1934. Novel dealing with the conflict in the lives of Easterners and Middle Westerners, in Boston, at the time of the Sacco-Vanzetti case.

*The World of Fiction.* Boston: Houghton Mifflin Company, 1934. DeVoto's attempt to set forth clearly his theories about fiction.

*The Writer's Handbook.* (With W. F. BRYAN and ARTHUR A. NETHERCOT.) New York: The Macmillan Company, 1928. Freshman English text, almost a museum piece; DeVoto was responsible for chapter on diction.

*The Year of Decision: 1846.* Boston: Little, Brown, and Company, 1943. Narrative of every event of importance in America in what DeVoto considered America's most crucial year.

## 2. Books Edited by Bernard DeVoto

*The Journals of Lewis and Clark.* Boston: Houghton Mifflin Company, 1953. Condensation of the journals of the famous expedition, with preface and introduction.

*Mark Twain in Eruption.* New York: Harper and Brothers, 1940. Anthology of Mark Twain's less cautious writing.

*The Portable Mark Twain.* New York: The Viking Press, 1946. Collection of Mark Twain's works with introduction by DeVoto; Southern friend, not intending a pun, commented that he did not believe Mark Twain could be "po'table."

## 3. Periodical Essays by DeVoto Used in this Book

Listing all of DeVoto's magazine articles would be impractical, for it has already been done in *Four Portraits* (see below). This list includes only those which I have used in pursuit of my thesis, but specific articles in the "Easy Chair" series are cited in the footnotes.

"The Anxious West," *Harper's Magazine*, CXCIII (December, 1946), 481-91.

"The Easy Chair," *Harper's Magazine*, CLXXI (November, 1935) to CCXI (January, 1956). A four-page, double-column essay appearing monthly.

"Main Street Twenty Years After," *Harper's Magazine*, CLXXI (November, 1940), 580-87.

"Sacred Cows and Public Lands," *Harper's Magazine*, CXCVII (July, 1948), 44-55.

"The West Against Itself," *Harper's Magazine*, CXCIV (January, 1947), 1-13.

"The West: A Plundered Province," *Harper's Magazine*, CLXXIX (August, 1934), 355-64.

## SECONDARY SOURCES

DeKay, Drake. "Manifest Destiny," *Encyclopedia Americana* (1964), XVIII, 218d. Gives the source of the phrase "manifest destiny."

*Four Portraits and One Subject: Bernard DeVoto*. Boston: Houghton Mifflin Company, 1963. Includes "The Historian," by Catherine Drinker Bowen; "The Writer," by Edith Mirrielees; "The Citizen," by Arthur M. Schlesinger, Jr.; "The Personality," by Wallace Stegner; and "A Bibliography of the Writings of Bernard DeVoto," by Julius P. Barclay, with the collaboration of Elaine Helmer Parnie.

Wilson, Edmund. "Complaints: II, Bernard DeVoto," *New Republic*, LXXXIX (February 3, 1937), 405-8.

Little else of value has been done on DeVoto, although in 1938 Garrett Mattingly prematurely published *Bernard DeVoto: A Preliminary Appraisal*, a work too early to be of real value for this study.

The sketches in *Four Portraits* are valuable personal evaluations. The bibliography is reliable and almost complete. Although the sketches contain minor errors, especially in dates, they are the best evaluations of DeVoto yet to appear in book form.

Since the work on this book was completed, two scholarly treatments of DeVoto's criticism have emerged from (or have been buried in) the academic bonepile: Melvin Gill's dissertation on DeVoto's criticism, New York University, 1964, which I have not seen, and Sara Catherine Sawey's master's thesis, "Bernard DeVoto and the Metaphysical Critics: The Book That Isn't There," University of Texas, 1966, which I have seen.

# Index

Maury, Matthew, 79
Meek, Joe, 85, 86
Meine, Franklin J., *Tall Tales of the Southwest*, 24, 37, 41, 45, 74
Melville, Herman, 64
*Moby Dick*, 40, 49
Mencken, H. L., 63, 101, 104-5, 128
Mexican War, 75, 83, 129
Miller, Alfred Jacob, 83, 84, 85
*Minority Report, see* DeVoto
Mirrielees, Edith R., 131
*Moby Dick, see* Melville
Montana's exploitation of natural resources, 116-17
Morgan, Dale, 93
Mormon Battalion, 75
"Mountain men," 83-89. List, 85
*Mountain Time, see* DeVoto
Muir, John, 82
Mumford, Lewis, 41, 101
Murfree, Mary Noailles, 128

*National Geographic Magazine*, 74
National Park Service, 118-22, 124
Neihdart, John G., 74
Nevins, Allan, 73
"New Criticism," 38, 47
New Deal, 109, 118
*New England Indian Summer, see* Brooks, Van Wyck
"New frontier," 110
Newell, Doc, 85
Norris, Frank, 64

Olympia National Park, 119
*Ordeal of Mark Twain, The, see* Brooks, Van Wyck
*Oregon Trail, The, see* Parkman

Paine, Albert Bigelow, 36
Parkman, Francis, 67, 75, 78, 82, 89
*The Oregon Trail*, 78
Parrington, Vernon Louis, 57-8
Paxson, Frederick, *History of the American Frontier*, 73, 74, 93
Perry, George Sessions, 128
Pike County man, 42
Pinchot, Gifford, *Breaking New Ground*, 122

Pioneer, the, 99-100, 102
Poe, Edgar Allan, 56, 82
Polk, James K., 79, 80
*Portable Mark Twain, The, see* DeVoto
Pound, Ezra, 68
Powell, John Wesley, 68, 69, 82
Private enterprise, 117
Public lands, struggle over, 112-27
Puritans and Puritanism, 102-3

Rabelais, 48
Range cattle industry, 115
Rebel yell, 82
*Redbook*, 35
Republican party, 123-25
Richards, I. A., 58
*Rise of Silas Lapham, The, see* Howells
Robinson, E. A., 64, 68
Roosevelt, Franklin D., 106
Roosevelt, Theodore, 122, 124
Ruxton, George F., 75, 85

Sacco-Vanzetti case, 29
Sandburg, Carl, 68, 102
*Saturday Evening Post*, 35, 96
*Saturday Review of Literature*, 18, 33, 35, 59, 61, 96
Schlesinger, Arthur M., Jr., 17, 74, 113, 116, 122, 129
"Seven Cities," 92
Sharpe, Cecil, 41
Soil Conservation, 113, 127
Spalding, Eliza, and Henry H., 86
Spanish Civil War, 105
Stassen, Harold, 123
Stearns, Harold, 101
Stegner, Wallace, 32, 75, 93, 131
Stewart, George, 93
Stewart, Sir William Drummond, 84, 85
Stowe, Harriet Beecher, 41
Strachey, Lytton, 53
Sublettes, 85
Sutter's Fort, 75
Swift, Jonathan, 48

*Index*